ISSUES OF CONSTITUTIONALISM

Musisi Stephen KASOZI

ISSUES OF CONSTITUTIONALISM
A case study of Uganda

Domuni-Press

2023

THIS BOOK IS PUBLISHED BY DOMUNI-PRESS
LAW COLLECTION

ISBN: 978-2-36648-179-2
© DOMUNI-PRESS, February 2023

Acknowledgments

I am very grateful to Prof Apollinaire Chishugi Thesis Supervisor for his guidance, Carly Wood Tutor for English-speaking students at Domuni University and all staff for academic support and timely response during the period of study. Tribute also goes to my fellow students who have been so willing to contribute, assist and work as a team when required. Thank you all for the effort.

Special tribute goes to Josephine Nakigudde who did everything possible to distribute questionnaires and interview transcripts on my behalf in Uganda when it was difficult for me to travel to Uganda. Thank you for organising the people I called and talked to over the phone although it was very difficult given the political environment at the time in Uganda. Thank you so much for returning the questionnaires and interview transcripts on time. Also not forgetting Allan Higgins our Managing Director at work who made sure that I enrolled on the course. Thank you so much and may God bless you all.

Abstract

Much as it is argued that constitutionalism promotes the rule of law, however, it is also argued that many African leaders do not believe in constitutional rule or those provisions that limit their powers. It is therefore argued that not every state that has a constitution (in that sense) is a constitutional state. On this basis, some are of the opinion that some are 'sham constitutions', in that they exist for 'cosmetic' purposes only and have no effect in reality. Since this debate is on-going, an inquiry has been carried out on negative implications of constitutional amendments intended for the benefit of incumbent leaders. The general objective of the study is that any Constitution designed in a constitutional democracy must promote constitutionalism and would protect democracy, the rule of law and constitutionalism. However, in some situations, it is not the case. The study, therefore, critically analysed the doctrine of constitutionalism in light of majoritarian democracies in Africa focusing on Uganda as the case study. A descriptive research method was used to gather information for this research aiming to look at the characteristics of the situation in Uganda. As a result of the study, it has been found that there is a distinction between 'democracy' and 'rule of law' based on the idea that democracy does not necessarily result into the 'rule of law'. It has also been found that the idea of a constitutional democracy as a system that can guarantee the rule of law is distorted, fraud and so much generalised. Democracy means much more than the participation of the people in elections and politics. The implication is that democracy and rule of law are both distinct and relative terms and in order to understand them clearly, much more need to be taken into consideration than a generalised value approach. Democracy, the constitution, the rule of law and constitutionalism are limited in applicability and therefore, a constitutional democracy cannot be 'the only way' or system.

Democracy, the constitution, and rule of law, and constitutionalism, therefore, should all be understood as living ideas and that they are capable of changing or evolving.

Keywords: The Constitution, Constitutional democracy, rule of law and constitutionalism.

General Introduction

Supposing someone takes clothes that belong to Peter and wears them, does the wearing of Peter's clothes make that individual Peter? This is exactly the question one needs to ask in regard with majoritarian democracies in Africa. African states from the time of independence, adopted constitutions as a way of governance taking from their colonial masters. The problem however is whether the existence of a written document a condition enough to satisfy that a state is a constitutional state. The exegesis of the problem is on the misunderstandings regarding the constitution as a written document, the rule of law, constitutional democracy, and constitutionalism. It is generally argued that a constitution that is designed to promote constitutionalism would protect the rule of law and guarantee the protection of human rights. What if a constitution as a written document exists in a given state, and yet those values are lacking?

This is exactly what is thought to be happening in many majoritarian democracies in Africa, such principles appear to be lacking or fraud. If democracy is about constitutionalism, one wonders why often a constitution as a set of rules, is something which politicians and political activists are always seeking either to change radically, modify, keep the same or, if they are revolutionaries, overthrow. According to current studies, it is argued that some of the constitutions in majoritarian democracies are a show case and therefore the area of concern for this study is that constitutions are often amended with the aim to keep incumbent leaders in power. This study is based on the current debates on the constitution, constitutional democracy, the rule of law and constitutionalism.

Limitations of the Research

This paper limits its research to constitutional amendments in Uganda and negative implications.

Background of Study

Historically, it is purportedly argued that western constitutionalism failed in the immediate post-colonial Africa, and it is the reason why many African states after Independence, adopted a trend of dictatorial regimes and/or one-party rule as an alternative. At the time, many African states were gaining independence in the 1960s, it was a time of competing political ideologies like communism, socialism, and capitalism. The pressure from both within and without forced African governments to re-establish their credibility by amending or radically changing their constitutions. There were different factors at play forcing independence leaders amending the independence constitutions. Some factors had to do with political ideologies of the time as some wanted to align themselves with communist and socialist countries. However, also, it is argued that many independence leaders amended constitutions of their countries in their favour to keep themselves in power. This kind of argument can be detected in Okoni Akiba's reasoning that:

> All African governments that acquired independence in the 1960's had constitutions that provided for the protection of human rights, separation of powers, and independent judiciary including parliamentary bodies. But within a few years the constitutions were abrogated, nullified, or rewritten. In some cases, single party structures were established, with the excuse that Western constitutional model cannot be expected to take root in Africa[1].

Depending on the available knowledge, it is evident that since independence from their colonial masters, many African states have gone through a lot of turmoil seeing constitutional provisions

---

[1] Okoni Akiba, "Constitutional Government and the Future of constitutionalism in Africa," in Constitutionalism and Society in Africa, ed. Okoni Akiba (Burlington: Ashgate Publishing Company, 2004), 3.

abrogated, amended, subverted, suspended, or brazenly ignored. This has not projected well in terms of democracy, rule of law and constitutionalism on the African continent. Many African leaders were or have been removed from power through military coups rather than through a general election and there are many examples of African leaders in the past and at present who would not leave power through a constitutional and democratic process of an election. This has resulted into negative implications in terms of democratisation, good governance, rule of law and constitutionalism on the continent.

It is believed that since the late twentieth century, has been an era of constitution making with issues of constitutionalism gaining considerable prominence on the continent. From the available information, the winds of change that started happening in the 1980's much as they generated expectations of a new dawn and an end of an era of corrupt, authoritarian, and incompetent dictatorships, that had earned the continent notoriety for political stability, civil wars, conflicts etc. the factors however that lead to constitutional instabilities in Africa have continued to haunt African democracies. What is disturbing is that the new wave of constitutionalism is not founded on the basis that there was an absence of the constitution as a written document in the affected countries, but possibly on other factors. But all the same, recent developments are constituting a new epoch in African history – the epoch of the rebirth assuming a new value within the context of debates about politics, constitutional democracy, the rule of law, and constitutionalism however, with new challenges.

One suggestion leading to the new wave of constitutional making, it is argued that since the 1980s, "donors have exerted pressure on African states to pursue neo-liberal economic and political reforms. Whereas donors initially put emphasis on economic reforms, they have since the 1990s added on political reforms arguing that the success of economic reforms is depended upon political factors which may include political stability or instability, corruption, bureaucracy etc. As a result, many African states embraced democratic governance even though with serious flaws"[2]. But since the introduction of political reforms, very little progress has been made in terms of democracy, the rule of law and constitutionalism. African leaders today hope and calculate that adoption of written constitutions will legitimize their regimes in several possible ways, as self-justification in the eyes of the world as a promise of just and democratic rule, and to their own citizens as a manifestation of consent and mutual respect. In their calculations, African leaders have assumed that the existence of a written Constitution means democracy, rule of law and constitutionalism before the donor nations.

The experiences under these new or revised constitutions in the last decade though have exposed numerous structural and institutional weaknesses and gaps. A few of what one can consider as some of the fundamental challenges that have made present constitutions not to stand the test of time. The recent constitutional changes, it is assumed, have failed to adequately draw inspiration from some silent lessons of Africa's dark authoritarian past. For example, little has been done to curb the temptation for leaders to seek to entrench themselves or their parties in office[3]. As result, the constitutional rights revolution on the continent, whilst real, remains uncertain. Executive power in Africa is still overwhelming partly because, the leaders do not believe in constitutional rule or those provisions that limit their powers and this is still a prevailing problem of which solutions need to be found and very urgently.

Problem of Study

As part of the problem, one of the arguments in current studies is that not every state that has a constitution (in that sense) is a constitutional state. Some arguing on this basis, are of a view that

---

[2] Muhumuza, "From Fundamental Change to No Change: The NRM and democratisation in Uganda," Journals Open Edition, http;//www.journals.openedition.org/east Africa/578 (accessed…)

[3] Charles, M. Fombad, "Challenges to Constitutionalism and Constitutional Rights in Africa and the enabling role of Political parties: Lessons and Perspectives from Southern Africa." The American Journal of Comparative Law (2007): 3.

some are façade/sham constitutions, in that they exist for 'cosmetic' purposes only and have no effect in reality. Given the background of this study, due to its importance, it is a subject that cannot be ignored by academicians and researchers to find solutions to deal with the problem. New developments in terms of research have raised questions as to the traditional understanding that the existence of a constitution as a written document is condition enough to satisfy that a state in question is indeed a constitutional state.

Kabumba a lecturer of constitutional law at Makerere University for-example argues citing the 1995 Uganda constitution as nothing, but an illusory law. It is mesmerising the way Kabumba uses strong language of the 1995 Uganda constitution. He further characterises the Ugandan constitution as an elaborate farce that is cynically perpetrated by the president to consolidate and extend his hold on power[4]. The argument as elsewhere is that in contemporary Africa, authoritarian leaders have evolved and moved to adopt a 'Constitution' as a show case for their continued hold on power but with no actual respect to democracy, the rule of law and constitutionalism.

Since constitutions have now come to be seen as mere fetishes that adorn rulers' offices, there is an assumption that even constitutional amendments to be undertaken in a constitutional democracy as part of the normal constitutional process, are now mostly hinged on political power consolidation, political party superiority, and the giving of the president ultimate power and authority whilst in office.

This has resulted in several serious implications especially negative ones which this study is trying to investigate. This is causing many people to question constitutional democracy and the entire project of constitutionalism as based on western democracy. People are starting to think of democracy in distinctive ways and asking questions as well. Does democracy result in the rule of law or the rule of law can exist without a democracy? What is more important: A

---

[4] Kabumba, Busingye. *Uganda at 50 and the problem of "sham constitutions."* Monitor Newspaper. Online, 24 September 2012.

capitalist democracy where a few are exorbitantly rich while the majority are poor and starving but with freedom of speech etc?

China as a communist and socialist country but with no track record of democratic principles and human rights, has in recent years managed to lift 98.99 million impoverished rural residents living under the current poverty line out of poverty[5]. Current debates are now questioning whether democracy can guarantee human rights. The questions being asked are whether the poor majority with no food, medicine, or proper housing in a democratic country like the USA have more human rights compared to people with a descent income, food, proper housing, medicine etc but living in China which is not a democratic state? The new debates are refocusing our attention to look again at the understanding of democracy, rule of law, good governance, and constitutionalism.

Since a constitution is interpreted by some as a social contract, this is the background of the problem because as a social contract, in a democracy, it is argued that it should have rules that equally apply to everyone since a person's moral and political obligations are dependent on it. However equal application has different meanings and can be understood in different ways. In a constitutional democracy like Kenya or Uganda, practically, would the rules apply equally in regard with political leaders as compared to an ordinary citizen from Mbale or Kiyambu? What about in the case of a constitutional monarchy like the UK, would the rules apply in the same way to the royal family as they would to a poor young black man born in the poor suburbs of South London? Equality before the law similarly may have different meanings at given situations.

The problem in majoritarian democracies in Africa is that it is argued that constitutionalism is a fallacy with deliberate abuse, misinterpretation, and manipulations resulting in political conflicts and electoral disputes but then, forced to function in a way as if it were not a fallacy. Although many of the majoritarian states in Africa have written documents as constitutions, but it appears that the rule of law is disregarded when it comes to democracy, constitutionalism

---

[5] Chaolan, Wu. "Has China lifted 100 million people out of poverty? Yes, it has!" *People's Daily Online*. 6 March 2021.

and respect of human rights as generally understood in western democracies. The rule of law is not disregarded in its totality as such, but deliberately manipulated to work for and benefit of those in power.

The argument that of recent there has been a revival of the idea of constitutional making and that a new wave of democratisation is sweeping through Africa can be received with mixed feelings. On one hand, it is undeniable that indeed there has been an effort around democratisation and constitution making, but on the other hand, whether the new wave is having a positive effect and meaning in terms of function ability.

Much as there has been a new wave of democratisation, there are still descending voices and Mutual is one of them holding the opinion that 'the last two decades of the twentieth century, Africa has witnessed a deepening crisis of government and statehood'[6]. This is part of the problem of this study and has implications on democracy, the rule of law and constitutionalism and it is perceived that these values are failing in Africa. Therefore, more research is needed to get to the proper understanding as to why there is this perceived failure regarding some African states.

Based on current studies, there are some scholars with a view that 'constitutions' in majoritarian democracies in Africa are in line with the political reality, but do not impose binding rules upon it; and that on the contrary, they reinforce government powers[7]. If constitutions are intended to reinforce government powers at the cost of the ordinary citizens, then the intended values and ideals of democracy have failed. Democracy means a government by the people. This is perceived as a problem, and Ekeh as one of the respected scholars, holds the same view as well when he asserts that in these circumstances, constitutions have become mere fetishes that adorn rulers' offices. What is required is a more fundamental

---

[6] See Mutual.

[7] See generally Loewenstein (1972, 174); Sartori (1962, 853); Murphy (1993A, 8-9); Law and Versteeg (2013, 863).

recognition that a constitution is a people's document[8]. The problem is that most of African constitutions do recognise that their constitutions are people's documents or at least in word.

The constitution in a constitutional democracy, is intended to serve the people and what leaders ought to do is to obey the constitution and other laws within the state. However, what is perceived as a problem, is that many of the African leaders tend to bend the rules to suit with what they want in the back of their minds believing that constitutions are there to serve them and not the other way round and this is a problem with serious implications. It is evident enough that across Africa even with a written document, many constitutions are still controlled, used, and abused by the powerful leaders.

The problem even goes further and based on current views and debates, there is an ongoing argument that whereas constitutions are usually designed to endure in order to ensure political stability, they are not immutable documents frozen in time that should endure regardless of the changes in the polity's circumstances and citizens' values. Many would argue that constitutional amendments are part of a democratic and constitutional process.

Scholars like Fombad hints on the existing problem as well when he points out that "because constitutions are inevitably obsolesced with time, there must be an effective and efficient process to ensure that they can be regularly updated to avoid the twin dangers of extra-legal or revolutionary methods of change on one hand and arbitrary, hasty and opportunistic changes on the other[9]." The problem is that the process of change or being updated has on many occasions often been abducted by selfish and greedy leaders with the intention of making the changes in their favour, but not for the promotion of the rule of law.

---

[8] Peter, P. Ekeh. "The Impact of Imperialism on Constitutional Thought in Africa in Constitutionalism and Society in Africa." *In Constitutionalism and society in Africa*, edited by Okoni Akiba, Ohio University: Ashgate, 2004, 38.

[9] Charles Manga Fombad. "Limits on the power to amend constitutions: Recent trends in Africa and their potential impact on constitutionalism". *World Congress of Constitutional Law*, Athens Greece: online, 11-15 June 2007, 28.

Constitutional debates are bringing new problems to the surface. At the moment, a good number of African thinkers are struggling to bring consensus to two opposing idealistic positions (i) Must a constitution establish a stable framework for the exercise of public power which is in some way fixed by factors like original public meaning or authorial intentions? (ii) Or should it be a living document which grows and develops in tandem with changing political values and principles? Striking a balance between the two, has proven to be a problem. On the first point, some would argue that it is meaningless to have a constitution that can be changed at any time and that cannot ensure political stability. There are also those who argue that the idea of the endurance of the constitution alone, cannot guarantee stability and itself can be a cause of instability. In a number of African states for-example, in situations where the constitution had shown stability or endurance, African leaders opted to amend, suspend, or discard the entire constitution.

Further, connected to the above, some have turned up to argue that it is important to have that provision of flexibility in the constitution since constitutions are not immutable documents frozen in time that should endure regardless of the changes. But the very idea of a living document, has been open to abuse by authoritarian leaders who moved to amend constitutions whenever they saw it necessary in their favour. Some scholars like Hutchinson and Colon-Rios for-example argued while referencing to Elkins, Ginsberg, and Melton that 'there are some real benefits for periodic constitutional replacement' but very much work from the definite assumption that 'a long life is better life' and that 'survival' is success.

Some scholars have highlighted constitutional problems in majoritarian democracies in Africa emanating from weak institutions. People like Cheeseman have argued that 'African legislatures and judiciaries are largely irrelevant because they are powerless to check the authority of the executive[10]. He further argues that to date, a significant proportion of the literature has depicted a continent in which formal institutions do not perform as intended; rather, official rules are described as being weak and fragile, rendered

---

[10] Nick, Cheeseman. "Institutions and Democracy: How the rules of the game shape political developments." *ResearchGate*, February 2018.

vulnerable to executive manipulation by the salience of corrupt personal networks and ethnic politics[11]. The problem is that in many African states, the rule of law has been manipulated to lead to the desired outcome by leaders and not as per rule of law as understood in a proper functioning constitutional democracy.

Elkins, Ginsburg, Melton[12] and others their insistence that a long-life expectancy is the best indicator of constitutional health is for a very good reason; the longer the constitution lives, the better the nation's constitutional health can be considered to be[13]. It is therefore assumed that if the constitutional process is hijacked by the executive, it has implications. By endurance, it is intended to mean a constitution that can offer stability without giving way. The concern of this paper, is to find solutions on how the dangers of constitutions being controlled, used, and abused by powerful leaders who want to overstay in power can be avoided. This is a real problem facing many 'constitutional' democracies in Africa and therefore, need proper investigation and the understanding of the implications attached. By clearly understanding the implications, it can positively lead to identifying relevant measures that can be taken in order to deal with the problem.

Although African leaders continue to seek to adopt written constitutions, however the problem is that most of them are still obsessed with the idea of 'too much centralised power' in their hands and often consider themselves 'as above the law' because they see themselves in light of former kings and as 'fathers of the nation' and that without them, the nation cannot survive. It is therefore assumed that this kind of behaviour by leaders in connection with the problems highlighted above, has serious negative implications. If the populace in African states had an idea of the seriousness of such implications, such a situation would not be allowed to happen or continue happening at any cost. But because of lack of knowledge and because not enough study has been done on such implications, there is still

---

[11] Ibid.

[12] See Elkins, Ginsberg, Melton, and Hutchinson.

[13] Allan C., Hutchinson, and Colon-Rios Joel. "Democracy, constitutionalism and Judicial Review." *A Journal of Social and Political Theory* (Berghahn Books) 58 (June 2011): p.45.

ignorance of the seriousness (cost) attached as a result of such implications.

Specific Problem

It is assumed that constitutional amendments intended for the benefit of incumbent leaders in majoritarian democracies in Africa has serious negative implications.

Justification of the Study

At the moment, it cannot be argued that based on the knowledge and information available on the constitution, constitutional democracy, rule of law and constitutionalism that the information is enough and therefore no more information is needed. The more study is conducted on a recurrent problem, the more we get to understand the problem. But also, it is important to understand that nothing remains the same over a very long period of time. Since society keeps changing, the needs of society also keep changing. It is therefore important to get new information to add on the existing information. Africa's situation has been changing for quite some time. Africa experienced a period of colonisation by colonial powers and many African states emerged in the 1960s as newly formed independent states. The new states emerged with new constitutions which many of them ended up discarded or suspended because the dynamics within the newly formed states were different from those of their former colonial masters. In many African states, nationalism and a one-party system ended up taking root.

Given the history of many African states, it is currently argued that Africans have a hangover with the one-party mentality narrative of which ruling elites use of constitutions is to control people rather than submit to the supremacy of the law. It is also argued that Africans, are still prisoners of the 'strongman syndrome' rather than the use or introduction of strong institutions to work for the common good and this, has implications on the survival of constitutionalism in Africa. As Cheeseman points out that the theme of the collapse of constitutional rule has become more prevalent[14]. Distorted conceptions of constitutionalism and the ideology of one party-rule have been used by segments of society to legitimise irresponsible behaviour of leaders and to frustrate public demands for the rule of law and democracy. Based on what is already known, it is clear that there is a knowledge gap as in regard to the proper understanding and making a distinction between the idea of having a constitution as a written document on one hand and having it as a functional constitution that can promote constitutionalism and the rule of law on the other.

Muhumuza for-example argues that "Uganda's post-independence period, like other African states, has been afflicted by authoritarian rule which has led to development crisis. He further points out that authoritarian African leaders accepted to undertake democratic reforms in order to access donor assistance but harboured a hidden agenda to manipulate them[15]. In the process, many of them have flouted democratic rules by amending constitutions, creating proxy parties, harassing the opposition, and organising flawed elections, among others. This, it is assumed has negative implications and the inquiry on negative implications is intended at increasing understanding on the nature of the problem and on this basis, the study is necessary.

Adding further to the justification of the study, recent studies indicate that many sub-Saharan countries have been impacted on by the new wave of political reforms but the challenges that has come with it, have not been properly researched and no solutions have been found as of yet. There is therefore a need for more research around democracy, the rule of law and constitutionalism looking at Africa's problems specifically and from an African perspective so as to understand better the problems leading to constitutional crises in Africa.

---

[14] Cheeseman, Nick. "Institutions and Democracy: How the rules of the game shape political developments." *Research Gate,* February 2018.

[15] Muhumuza. *From Fundamental Change to No Change: The NRM and democratisation in Uganda* [online], Available at: https://journals.openedition.org/eastafrica/578, 1 September 2009, 1.

It has been assumed by some that the answer to Africa's problems is thus not in democracy neither in constitutional making. This is a very radical suggestion; however, the underlying argument is that if it were so, African states by now would have made progress in regard with the rule of law and constitutionalism and it makes good sense. Therefore, issue of constitutionalism remains a problem in majoritarian democracies in Africa. Much of the information available, relates to western democracies and has limited relevance when it comes to the challenges faced by many of the African states even if the understanding of constitutionalism is to be considered a universal concept.

It is also argued that the need for African leaders to adopt written constitutions today is not because of constitutionalism and the rule of law, but rather it is a way that they can legitimise their regimes in several possible ways, as self-justification in the eyes of the world as a promise of just and democratic rule, and to their own citizens as a manifestation of consent and mutual respect as already indicated above. Based on these assumptions and since, there is lack of sufficient knowledge in relation to the problem, it is necessary to do a study. The study will therefore critically analyse what is meant by democracy, the constitution, rule of law and constitutionalism considering African constitutional and majoritarian democracies. Since this debate is on-going, there is a need for more research around democracy, the rule of law and constitutionalism from an African perspective so as to add to the available knowledge and also try to bridge the knowledge gap.

As already indicated above, from the 1990's, a new wave of democratisation swept through the African continent. And with it came a new form of 'constitutional-making' with the aim to ditch dictatorial regimes and one-party rule. A number of African states revised their constitutions to contain some provisions that seem to recognise and protect most of the fundamental human rights that are associated with democratic governance and constitutionalism.

However, given what is happening on the ground in many of the African states, it is believed that there is rampant abuse of human rights, and the idea of the rule of law is questionable. The problem can be traced in the argument that Western constitutional model cannot take root in Africa. At the same time, African leaders still continue on the path of constitution making and one wonders the rationale behind it. Is it done for the rule of law or for cosmetic show purposes? Some have even suggested that we are now seeing in some perceived constitutional states, autocratic kingdoms emerging on the continent. Since it is argued that the dynamics in the African democracies are different from western democracies, more study is therefore needed.

Africa has so many examples of leaders who have been in power for decades and overthrown by means of military coup/s and the one of the recent examples is that of Robert Mugabe who came into power at the time of Zimbabwe's independence, clung to power and overthrown only recently in the military coup. This has the implication that independence constitutions failed to result into functional democracy, the rule of law and constitutionalism which in turn has further negative implications that need to be investigated. This paper, therefore, is deeply concerned with mainly the negative implications of constitutional amendments intended to benefit incumbent leaders and this is the central problem of this study.

The problem is extended further in the sense that more people are now beginning to believe that the existence of a written document is not condition enough to satisfy that a state is a constitutional state. On other hand, there is still an insistence by yet some that the existence of a written document is condition enough to satisfy that a state is a constitutional state. More research is therefore needed in order to shed more light on the subject.

Under the constitution, there are certain instances, whereby it is possible to have misunderstandings as to 'who actually owns the constitution' in a majoritarian democracy. It is clear that there is a knowledge gap the way African people understand or interpret democracy, the rule of law and constitutionalism. So far, no literature has adequately provided a solution to the problem and on that basis, more knowledge is needed. In addition, because of lack of adequate knowledge, no real measures have been put in place to address the problem although there is some progress made with new studies being conducted on democracy, the rule of law and constitutionalism in Africa.

This study is justified on the basis that although there exists a wealth of literature on the implication of constitutional amendment in majoritarian democracies generally, but the literature available appear not to address the problem in the African context. There is also an apparent scarcity regarding the treatment of the problem that this paper seeks to address. The inquiry on negative implications is intended at increasing understanding and contributing to knowledge in the context of debates about philosophy of law, the constitution as a document, the rule of law, constitutionalism, politics, statehood, and democracy considering majoritarian democracies in Africa. Uganda has been chosen because it provides a very good case study of constitutional amendments intended for the benefit of incumbent leaders and their dominant parties and can provide us with a very good sample for the rest of Africa. Next, the paper will now focus on the problem of this study.

Aims and Objectives

The aim of this study is to identify the negative implications of constitutional amendments aimed at the benefit of leaders in majoritarian democracies in Africa and what can be done or the measures that can be taken to address the problem.

General Objective

The general objective is that any Constitution designed in a majoritarian democracy must promote constitutionalism and would protect the rule of law and therefore this study will critically analyse the doctrine of constitutionalism in light of majoritarian democracies in Africa and how the legislature and executive organs have influenced constitutional amendments in favour of the incumbent.

Specific Objectives

1) To critically analyse whether the existence of a written constitution a condition enough to satisfy that Uganda is a constitutional state.

2) To consider whether a constitutional democracy like Uganda, can promote constitutionalism.

3) To investigate whether the legislature have indeed influenced constitutional amendments in Uganda in favour of the executive.

4) To investigate the negative implications of constitutional amendments in Uganda.

Research question

What are the negative implications of constitutional amendments intended for the benefit of incumbent leaders in majoritarian democracies in Africa?

Sub-Questions

1) Is a written a Constitution condition enough to satisfy that Uganda is a constitutional state?

2) Can a constitutional democracy like Uganda be able to promote constitutionalism?

3) What is the role of the legislature in constitutional amendments in Uganda and who are they aimed to favour?

Hypothesis

This research proceeds on the main presumption that constitutional amendments intended for the benefit of incumbent leaders in majoritarian democracies in Africa have serious negative implications. Further, it presumes that constitutionalism must be given a wider understanding in accordance with the dynamics of the society, the interpretation should not among others be sought to look only at a government with a constitution or a government established according to the constitution, but rather a government acting in accordance with the constitution is more important in all aspects but also not forgetting acting in the interest of the people. The Hypothesis will either be proved or disapproved during the study conducted.

Assumptions guiding the study

1) It is assumed that some constitutional amendments in Uganda are mostly hinged on political power consolidation, political party superiority, and giving the president ultimate power and authority whilst in office.

2) It is also assumed that some constitutional amendments made by parliament are mostly influenced by the executive arm of government.

3) It is also assumed that some constitutional amendments have belittled the leadership of Uganda and some other majoritarian democracies in Africa and have also bred a new regime of unlawful and un procedural administration.

Scope of the Study

The study is intended to evaluate the idea of the Constitution, democracy, rule of law, and the doctrine of constitutionalism. The study is intended to look most specifically the laws and procedure regulations of constitutional amendments and its implications. This research concerns the nature and scope of the power to amend constitutions and in whose interest. "Constitution" in this research is used to denote the narrow sense of the term, i.e., the cluster of supreme principles and rules, typically set in a written legal document (or a set of such documents), which establish and regulate the state's basic institutional arrangements and practices and express the nation's most enduring values[16].

Geographical Research

The study is being carried out in Uganda with an insightful juxtaposition to other African states.

---

[16] For wide and narrow senses of constitutions see Perry (2001, 103); Tully (2002, 204-5); Elkins, Ginsberg, and Melton (2009, 38-51).

The first chapter has attempted to introduce the study by giving an insight of the background, the problem, significance, or justification of the study, aims and objectives, and the questions the study is aiming to answer. The chapter has stated an assumption of the study and the scope of the study in terms of data collection. The next chapter will review the related literature.

Constitution

Literature Review

The previous Chapter, generally introduced the study, highlighted the background and justification of study, statement of the problem, aims and objectives, research questions, hypothesis, and scope of study. This chapter will now review the related literature on the historical background of the constitution, rule of law, constitutional democracy, the concept of the Constitution and constitutionalism, the idea of who owns the constitution, how constitutionalism questions are different from constitutional questions, a brief overview of constitutional interpretation and constitutional amendments and a brief conclusion of the chapter.

Although there exists a mammoth of literature on the aspect of constitutionalism and constitutional amendments in majoritarian democracies in Africa and the world at large, this paper seeks to add on the existing literature. However, many important aspects of this paper, relating to both form and substance, have been crafted with heavy reliance being placed on the existing literature. The first guiding question of the challenges facing majoritarian democracies in Africa today is: "Does the existence of a written constitution a condition enough to satisfy that a majoritarian democracy is a constitutional state?"

Historical Background of the Constitution

To have a reasonable reflection on the question, one need to understand the constitution and its historical background. When it comes to the 'Constitution', there are different opinions as to when the idea came into existence. Some would date it back to the city-states of ancient Greece. Reference is made to Aristotle (834 -322

B.C.) when he described a Constitution as 'creating a frame upon which the government and laws of a society are built'[17]. However, the new idea of the constitution and constitutionalism can be traced back in 1215 to King John of England when he was forced by a group of wealthy nobles to sign a document called the Magna Carta which set certain limits on the king's power. It was the first document to put into writing that the king and his government were not above the law. Also, notable political philosopher Aristotle said more than two thousand years ago, "The rule of law is better than that of any individual." Lord Chief Justice Coke quoting Bracton said in the case of Proclamations (1610) 77 ALL.ER 1352, English Laws: "The King himself ought not to be subject to man, but subject to God and the law, because the law makes him King". The Magna Carta sought to prevent the king from exploiting his power and placed limits of royal authority by establishing law as power in itself.

According to the Law teacher, Edward Coke is said to be the originator of the concept 'Rule of Law' when he said that the king must be under God and Law and thus vindicated the supremacy of law over the pretentions of executives. Law therefore he said is perceived as more powerful and higher than the kings and there is nothing higher than the law because in its powers the weak shall prevail over the strong and justice shall triumph[18]. Despite royal absolutism, Brand also quoted the same statement and continued to say that then it became manifest that the natural law, the abstract, had fused with natural rights, the concrete[19]. Natural law was perceived as an abstract because the early thinkers referred to it as 'unwritten law' and a body of 'moral principles' common to all. The idea is that we conform to natural law for the good of society.

According to Amartya, Democracy as we know it today took a long time to emerge. From the signing of the Magna Carta in 1215 to the French and the American Revolutions in the eighteenth century, to the widening of the franchise in Europe and North America in the nineteenth century, democracy was not perceived as a normal form

---

[17] See Aristotle.

[18] Origin and Concept of Rule of Law. Prod. *Free Law essays*. Lawteacher.net, 23 July 2019.

[19] Brand James T. *"Natural Law and Constitutional Democracy"* (The Phi Beta Kappa Society) 5, no 1 (Winter 1936): p.7.

of government[20]. It was in the twentieth century that democracy became established as the 'normal' form of government to which any nation is entitled whether in Europe, America, Asia, or Africa. But for the system to run effectively, it had to be built on a firm foundation of a supreme document known as the constitution.

Apart from the Magna Carta, the first well detailed constitution was written during the summer of 1787 in Philadelphia, Pennsylvania by fifty-five delegates to a constitutional convention that was called to amend the articles of confederation (1781 – 89) in USA. Walubiri therefore is of a view that in the eighteenth century, the idea of constitutionalism came to be identified with a written Constitution[21]. The constitution in the first significance comprises of elements such as laws, theories, and interpretations that perform what is traditionally understood as "constitutional" functions. The second significance of the constitution refers to the formal written charter, a form that is now nearly universal among modern states. The idea of a 'Constitution' having been born and ready to take root, the Constitution had to be based on certain principles. The American constitution for example, was based on three primary principles: inherent rights, government by the people, and separation of powers.

The Constitution

The most commonly used definition of the term constitution refers to a set of rules and principles that define the nature and extent of government. Others like Barnett define the Constitution as a body of both (or either) written or unwritten rules not only governing the exercise and distribution of state authority, but also governing the relationship between organs of state and, also between organs of state and legal subjects[22]. Heffernan and Thompson are of a view that the

---

[20] Sen, Amartya. "Democracy as a Universal Value." *Journal of Democracy* 10, no.2 (1999): 3 – 17.

[21] Peter Mukidi Walubiri. "Liberating African Civil Society: Towards a New Context of Citizen Participation and Progressive Constitutionalism: *In constitutionalism in Africa: Creating opportunities, Facing Challenges*, by J. Oloka-Onyango, Kampala: Fountain Publishers, 2001, 84.

[22] See, D. Markwell. *Constitutional Conventions, and the Headship of State: Australian Experience.* Queensland: Connor Court Publishing, 2016, p.9.

constitution defines the relationship between the state and society, between actors who rule and citizens who are ruled. It also sets out how the state operates, which institutions comprise it and how they relate to one another[23]. According to Oloka-Onyango, written law includes the Constitution, Acts of Parliament, and subsidiary legislation.

While unwritten law includes laws, whose principles are not recognised but not written anywhere e.g., Common Law, and Customary Law. Written Law however takes precedence over unwritten Law[24]. A Constitution is considered as a fundamental system of law in any sovereign state. Constitution in the first sense of the word refers to the nature of a country with reference to its political conditions. Constitution in the second sense refers to the law that concerns itself with the establishment and exercise of political rule[25]. A constitution therefore consists of laws and norms that establish and empower highest organs of government – executive, legislature, and judiciary.

Jubril reasoned that the Constitution prescribes rights, responsibilities, obligations, and duties. It distributes, secures, and limits authority and powers, aggregates, and articulates aspirations and interests and outlines procedures for actions, and interactions and sanctions default[26]. Olasunkanmi thinking in terms of the supremacy of the law, argues that the constitution is supposed to be higher than anybody of legal regulations in human society[27]. According to Article 2 of the 1995 Uganda Constitution, the Constitution is the supreme law of the land and as such every enactment and judicial decision

---

[23] Richard Heffernan. "Governing at the centre: the politics of parliamentary state." *In Politics and Power in UK*, edited by Richard Heffernan and Grahame Thompson, 5 – 40. Milton Keynes: Edinburgh University Press, 2005.

[24] Joe Oloka-Onyango. "An Overview of the Legal System in Uganda." *Presentation at the China-Africa Legal Forum. Makerere University:* ResearchGate, 31 May 2020. 5.

[25] Dieter Grimm (2016, 142). *Constitutionalism: Past, Present, and Future.* Oxford University Press.

[26] B.M., Jubril. *Concept, Theory and Evolution of constitution concept constitutionalism and national Question: Centre for constitutionalism and demilitarization,* Lagos, 2000, P. 16.

[27] Olasunkanmi A. *Constitution without constitutionalism: interrogating the Africa experience.* Art Human Open Acc. J. 2018;2(5):272–276. DOI: 10.15406/ahoaj.2018.02.00069

must conform to the Constitution[28]. De Smith & Brazier[29], both reasoned that a constitution is primarily about political authority and location of power, conferment, distribution, exercise and limitation of authority and power among the agents of a state. According to the Wikipedia, most constitutions also attempt to define the relationship between individuals and the state, and also establish the broad rights of individual citizens[30]. Constitutions usually determine the limits of governmental authority and regulate interactions between the state and the country's citizens.

Tumwine while quoting Professor Dicey argued that constitutions in Commonwealth Africa provide for the supremacy of the constitution and that they further provided that any law which conflicts with the constitution would have no legal force[31]. Any law that conflicts with a constitution is deemed to be unconstitutional and can be declared by the judiciary as null and void in part or its wholeness e.g., the Uganda Referendum Act (in 2000), section of the Divorce Act 9 (in 2005), and the most recent Uganda Anti-homosexuality Act.

It is therefore important to bear in mind that customs are only valid if they are consistent with the constitution. For example, the courts in Uganda have declared practices such as female mutilation (FGM) as unconstitutional. However, Customary law which does not offend the constitution is considered upheld. In Uganda, the Constitution is the supreme law of the land and has binding effect and all legislation must conform to the constitution[32]. This means that Uganda is a constitutional republic as opposed to being governed under a parliamentary system of government. According to Heffernan and Thompson, the rules of procedure by which governments operate differ according to the particular form of

---

[28] See the 1995 Uganda Constitution.

[29] Brazier, De Smith, and Rodney. *Constitutional and Administrative Law*. London and New York: Penguin Book. P. 1977, 6 -7.

[30] Wikipedia.

[31] Grace Patrick, Tumwine-Mukubwa. "Ruled from the Grave: Challenging Antiquated constitutional doctrines and values in Commonwealth Africa." *In constitutionalism in Africa: creating opportunities, facing challenges*, edited by J. Oloka-Onyango, p. 287.

[32] Joe Oloka-Onyango. "An Overview of the Legal System in Uganda." *Presentation at the China-Africa Legal Forum*. Makerere University: ResearchGate, 31 May 2020. 3.

democracy or political regime. Presidential/parliamentary systems and federal/unitary systems present distinct constitutional arrangements at the governmental centre[33]. Grimm therefore argues that every political unit is constituted, but not everyone of them has a constitution. The term 'Constitution' covers both conditions, but the two are not the same. It is important to make a distinction between a government with a constitution and constitutionalism and a government with a constitution without constitutionalism. Every political system has a constitution whether it is a constitutional system or not. Instances of constitution without constitutionalism can be seen and evidenced in Uganda today.

The central idea of the constitution are the functions of the constitution and a functional constitution is sometimes referred to as the constitutional order or the "small-c" constitution. However, ordinary citizens in most countries including Uganda, what they think of when they hear the word constitution to be the founding charter which is the nominal or written constitution regardless of whether the document adequately serves the functions or its purposes. This is sometimes referred to as the "large-c" Constitution. It is a component or part of constitutionalism. By constitution we mean the means by which to achieve constitutionalism.

Since the constitution gives powers to the state to function as a state, Grimm opinions that the legally binding character of the constitution primarily concerns the power of the state. However, private persons are not the objects, but rather the beneficiaries of its provisions. To this extent, the constitution is based on the delineation between the state and the private sphere. Actors or forms of actions that do not conform to this division pose problems for the constitution[34]. It is therefore important to understand that every actor is subject to the higher law. In many states of the world, the higher law is the Constitution of the land.

In history, the Roman constitution for-example as according to Polybius consisted of rules supported by laws which in turn were

---

[33] Richard Heffernan, 12.

[34] Thomas, Paine. *Rights of Man, Common sense, and other political writings*. Edited by mark Philip. New York: Oxford University Press, 1998, 302.

supported by religion. In the Classical period, a period dominated by the Ancient Greeks and Romans, Socrates argued that 'law is a product of correct reasoning' and Plato said that 'Ultimate justice is discoverable through reason'. This is very important for any law including the constitution itself to be able to function.

Any society to function, there is a need for some sort of law either through custom, written, or unwritten principles. Depending to Tumwine's perspective, a constitution must declare the principles by which those organs must operate. Such a document must also embody specific values of societies should be controlled in order that it should not itself be destructive of the values it was intended to promote[35]. Constitutions organise, distribute, and regulate state power[36]. They set out the structure of the state, the major state institutions, and the principles governing their relationship with each other and with the state's citizens and provides for the independence of each organ.

A written constitution therefore is found in a legal document duly enacted in the form of laws like the 1995 Uganda constitution or any other constitution of any other state. An unwritten constitution consists of principles of the government that have never been enacted in the form of laws as in the case of the United Kingdom. On this basis, Aristotle, perceived law whether written or unwritten as 'Universal and immutable standards discoverable through reason and man-made law should conform to these standards.'

Wade & Bradley quoted Bolingbroke who in 1733 stated that "by Constitution, we mean whenever we speak with propriety and exactness that assemblage of laws, institutions and customs, derived from certain fixed principles of reason.... that compose the general system according to which society hath to be governed[37]. The laws or fixed principles of reason serve as a norm of conduct for government and citizens alike and act as a guidance of acceptable

---

[35] Grace Patrick, Tumwine-Mukubwa. "Ruled from the Grave: Challenging Antiquated constitutional doctrines and values in Commonwealth Africa." *In constitutionalism in Africa: creating opportunities,* facing challenges, edited by J. Oloka-Onyango, p. 287.

[36] Section 6(1) HRA.

[37] A.C. Wade & Bradley (1993, 4). *Constitutionalism and Administrative Law,* (11th. Ed.), London and New York: Longman.

behaviour. Tumwine quotes Wheare that in the narrow sense the constitution refers to a document having special legal sanctity and setting out the framework and the principal functions of the organs of government.

In a wider sense, it refers to the whole system of government of a country, the collection of rules which establish and regulate or govern the government[38]. Cicero's proclamation as quoted by Brand that natural law became the keystone of Stoic arch and from it emanated the unifying influence of '*jus gentium*' that 'law which natural reason established among all mankind is observed equally by all peoples[39]' and this is the basis of the fundamental law – the constitution and other laws as established came to be of great importance and hence talk of the rule of law. In essence, the law is the foundation of a constitutional democracy, and this leads to the theory of the supremacy of the constitution.

Theory of supremacy of the constitution (Constitutional theory)

Figures 1 below illustrates the supremacy theory of the constitution and within it is the idea of the separation of powers whereby powers are separated among different branches/arms of government. With the idea of separation of powers, each arm/branch has certain primary responsibilities for certain functions such as legislative, executive, and judicial functions. But the powers must be independent. The powers of one branch, must not be in conflict with the powers of the other branches. From the African perspective, the constitution can be seen figuratively as a pot of stew cooking on three separated, but equally important stones in the balancing of the pot so that the stew can continue to cook. However, if one of the stones is removed, the pot containing the soup is most likely to tip over. The three stones can as well represent the executive, legislature, and the

---

[38] Tumwine-Mukubwa, Grace Patrick. "Ruled from the Grave: Challenging Antiquated constitutional doctrines and values in Commonwealth Africa." *In constitutionalism in Africa: creating opportunities, facing challenges*, edited by J. Oloka-Onyango, p. 287.

[39] Brand, James T. "Natural Law and constitutional Democracy". The American Scholar (The Phi Beta Kappa Society)5, no.1 (Winter 1936), P. 6.

Judiciary. If any one of the constitutional democracy bases is removed, or fail to function, the idea of constitutionalism and rule of law can as well fail. This confirms the idea of the role that the three arms (Executive, Legislature and Judiciary) of government play in ensuring that the functionality and supremacy of the Constitution is upheld. The idea of separation of powers will be discussed further below. However, it is important to look at the illustration in figure 1 below. It is important to take note that the 'Constitution' is positioned on top of all other state institutions.

Figure 1

```
                      ┌──────────────┐
                      │ Constitution │
                      └──────┬───────┘
         ┌───────────────────┼───────────────────┐
         ▼                   ▼                    ▼
 ┌──────────────┐   ┌──────────────┐   ┌──────────────┐
 │  Executive   │   │ Legislature  │   │  Judiciary   │
 └──────────────┘   └──────────────┘   └──────────────┘
```

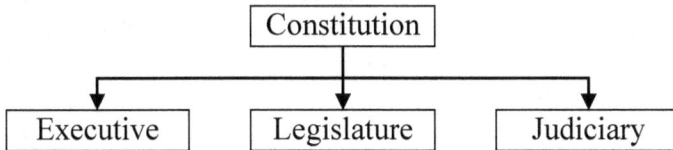

Based on figure 1, the idea is that a 'Constitution' is the 'supreme law of the land' and according to this theory, the constitution is sovereign and above everyone and every institution. The concept describes a constitution's ability to establish a hierarchical primacy within the sources of law and that everyone in that state must obey that supreme law is common among many theorists. Constitutional theory therefore can be described as an area of constitutional law that focuses on the underpinnings of a constitutional government.

Holmes argued that the constitution as the higher law, 'is a device for limiting the power of government…it disempowers short sighted majorities in the name of binding norms'[40]. Some thinkers are of a view that it is an impossible task exercising direct democracy in which everyone can participate in the making of laws, therefore, representation is important. It is possible in a direct democracy, the rights of the minorities to be taken away and end up being abused therefore, it is always important to have laws in place to protect

---

[40] Stephen, Holmes. *Passions and Constraint: On the theory of Liberal democracy*: Chicago University Press., 1995.p.135.

minority rights. Sometimes, direct democracy can result into what is called a tyranny of the majority and anyone not part of that majority would end up suffering. It is sometimes argued that the truth is not all on one side. Much as lack of democracy and authoritarian leaders can be accused of tyranny, it is as well possible for a democracy to be a tyranny of the masses.

The complexities of direct democracy are many and we know even Greece gave up on direct democracy. Imagine if everyone participated in the making of laws and the chaos that can come as a result of it. Madison in Loveland saw this problem and suggested that the dangers of faction could be reduced by adopting a form of 'representative government', in which laws would be made not directly by the people themselves, but by representatives the people had chosen to exercise law-making power on their behalf in a legislative assembly[41]. The reason direct democracy is not possible in modern societies is because it comes with high costs and risks.

It is for the above reason as to why professional representation is important, in addition to an established law in form of a constitution to protect the rights of the minorities. Uganda for example has done well regarding women and people with disabilities representation. Women and disabled representatives are elected to represent the interest group as opposed to direct democracy. As in the case of Uganda, to a reasonable extent, have increased the chances of interest groups to have their own representatives who could not have made it to parliament in a direct democracy.

In a direct democracy, the reason of having a body of professional representatives like parliament, is because it can arrive at decisions quicker than short sighted majorities. The logistics to get everybody on board can be challenging as well. But room must be left for direct elections and referendums where necessary and where representation cannot solve the matter at hand for example if the matter requires a referendum. Switzerland despite being considered as a role model of direct democracy in modern society, applies indirect democracy instead. In any constitutional democracy, power

---

[41] Ian Loveland. "*Constitutional Law, Administrative Law, and Human Rights.* Sixth Edition. Oxford: Oxford University Press, 2012, p. 10.

is a necessity as government is assigned the duty of impartial referee or umpire, enforcing societal rules against assault, murder, robbery, and fraud. All human relationships in a constitutional democracy are based on mutual consent and voluntary association and exchange.

The supremacy of the constitution is that it is positioned on top of all state institutions and businesses, making it a legal and political reality. Hague sees a constitution as a 'state code in which the powers of, and relationships between institutions are specified in considerable detail'[42]. Loveland perceived the notion of a constitution as some form of 'contract' negotiated either among the citizenry and their rulers, was not a novel idea, if only in philosophical terms, in 1776[43].

Jean-Jacques Rousseau had explored the concept of 'direct democracy' through an idealised small city state, in which all citizens participated personally in fashioning of laws under which they lived. In such a society, the legitimacy of all laws would rest on citizenry's constant, express consent to the process of government[44]. In a modern society, such a system maybe thought to be unpractical. Therefore, representation in form of parliament, or any other body appear to solve the problem of trying to get everyone on board in the process of making laws. Which can cause stagnation and decisions not made in good time. But once the law is made, it is supreme and everyone including the governors must obey that law.

Rousseau's central argument in the social contract therefore is that government attains the right to exist and to govern by consent of the governed. The initial consent could be through a general election in which every adult who qualifies can participate. Rousseau further argued that social order resulted from agreements between every individual citizen and the citizenry as a whole, from which government was formed. All government action therefore had a 'contractual' base; the citizens' rights and obligations under their

---

[42] Hague et al. 1993. P.262.

[43] Ian Loveland. *"Constitutional law, Administrative law, and Human Rights."* Third Edition. London. Lexis Nexis Butterworths, 2003, 4-5.

[44] Ian Loveland, 4-5.

constitution derived from covenants that they willingly made[45]. In any functional democracy, the consent of the majority and the rights of the minority, both must be protected by law.

The constitution therefore plays a very important role in any democracy because it is the contract or covenant on which society is governed. McMillan is of a view that the theory is important to justify the power that law enforcement can exert over the population as a whole[46]. In any constitutional democracy, citizens have an important role to play in the way they are governed and must give their consent.

Mutunga cites Lloyd and Freeman when they argue that social contract is wholly formal and analytic construct that can be used as a means of presenting conflicting political ideals[47]. For-example, when people elect their leaders, the majority form the government and the minority form the opposition to hold government to account. However, this system or arrangement works if the constitution and rule of law is respected. But without a commitment to a higher law, the state can operate for the short-term benefit of those in power, or the current majority. Those outside of the power circle, may find themselves unprotected, which in turn may make them more likely to resort to extra constitutional means or methods of demanding their rights or securing power.

Lloyd and Freeman in liberalism, refer to this as a theory either in terms of consent or as John Rawl called it the theory of justice[48]. John Locke however still maintains that society was subject to a form of natural or divine law which imposed limits on individual behaviour. The idea is that it is not possible to regulate on everything and society to function well, requires much more than what is prescribed within the law. Government exists to provide mechanisms for enforcing the substance of such natural law, the terms of which would serve as the constitution within which the government

---

[45] Ian Loveland, 4-5.

[46] See C. Bertram. "Rousseau and the Social Contract". 2003.

[47] Willy, Mutunga. "Constitutions, Law and Civil Society: Discourses on the legitimacy of people's power." *In constitutionalism in Africa: Creating opportunities*, facing challenges, by J. Oloka-Onyango, Kampala: Fountain Publishers, 2001, 134.

[48] Willy, Mutunga, 134.

operated[49]. Natural laws act as reference for 'positive laws' including the constitution as the supreme and primary source of law of which every citizen has to abide with; and this includes both the governors and the governed.

As in line with natural law arguments, Constitutions generate a set of inalienable principles and more specific provisions to which future law and government activity more generally must conform. Madison and other architects of the constitution however, rejected the Lockean notion of 'divine' law in the sense of considering human beings subservient to a rigid set of rules emanating from a deity. Similarly, they were not persuaded that the moral values which they wished to control the government of their new nation should be subject to an eternally fixed code of 'natural law, which would never be altered. Constitutional change and the idea of a living constitution is therefore important and central in the minds of many modern thinkers.

Thinkers with the above perspective, argue for a living constitution that can change as society evolve and change. Nevertheless, sceptics concluded that once they had succeeded in identifying the mutually acceptable principles according to which the foundations of government should be laid, those fundamental laws should enjoy considerable fixity. The idea is that the constitution must have the ability to withstand any shocks and pressures. For the American constitutional framers, the moral principles expressed in the constitution had not been lightly arrived at: they were not to be lightly discarded; they were not to be left at the mercy of ordinary institutions of government[50]. Therefore, the idea of a more fixed law in form of a grounded constitution appears to be more appealing and more likely to solve the problem.

Another line of thinking is the one defended by Thomas Hobbes and John Locke which is the notion of constitutionally unlimited sovereignty and in it we are confronted with a lot of problems because if one has a constitutionally unlimited sovereign,

---

[49] Ian, Loveland. *"Constitutional law, Administrative law, and Human Rights."* Third Edition. London. Lexis Nexis Butterworths, 2003, 5.

[50] Ian, Loveland, 16.

it is not possible to refer to the idea of limited government let alone speak of constitutionalism. Based on such problems, Hobbes in a way rejected the idea of constitutionalism and was in favour of unrestricted power in the hand of Leviathan. With the term Leviathan, Hobbes meant when individual members renounce their powers to execute the laws of nature.

From an African perspective, the theory of constitutionalism has been criticized for being too legalistic, for dwelling almost exclusively on constitutionally prescribed authority, and for ignoring or downplaying the importance of social forces in the study of politics. Many stigmatize the principles of constitutionalism for their overt normative content[51]. Africans believe that there more to the law. It is impossible to regulate on every situation and this where the idea of 'Ubuntu' comes in as a value and way of life.

Confronted with the complexities of Africa, one wonders if it is possible to argue in similar ways like Rousseau that the legitimacy of government and of all laws rest on the citizenry's constant express of consent to the process of government! Constant consent then becomes a controversial idea. Does it mean consent through an election or consent on every law that need to be passed? If one thinks of the people as sovereign, one may constantly find himself in a paradoxical situation of trying to get consent on every given decision-making situation which in most cases can be compared to someone trying to fetch water in a basket full of holes. There will always be dissenting voices. In a constitutional democracy, it is necessary to have majority rule, but it is also equally necessary to respect minority rights as coded into law.

The African situation provides us with a complication of which Okoth Ogenda referred to as a paradox that in case of a constitution as a people's document, 'instead of controlling a government, the constitution is there to serve government hence leaving room for manipulation'[52]. The idea that the constitution is a people's document under these circumstances makes no sense. It is no longer a people's

---

[51] Akiba, Okoni. "In search of Constitutional Order. *In Constitutionalism and Society in Africa*, by Okoni Akiba. Ohio University: Ashgate Publishing Ltd., 2004, p. 6.

[52] See Okoth Ogenda.

document, but rather a tool used by those in office to protect themselves and the power they hold from the people.

In cases where the law fails to function properly, the African 'Ubuntu' philosophy or way of life fills the void. Mokgoro reasons that Ubuntu philosophy represents personhood, humanity, humanness, and morality; a metaphor that describes group solidarity where such group solidarity is central to the survival of communities with scarcity of resources[53]. The maxim of Ubuntu philosophy is 'I am because you are.' One does not need to have a law, but these are principles in the African people's cultures which they have learnt over time as a way of life.

Mokgoro quoting Mazrui observes that, '…. Africa can never go back completely to its pre-colonial starting point, but there may be a case for re-establishing contacts with familiar landmarks of modernisation under indigenous impetus[54]. Given the failings of constitutionalism in Africa, this could be a wakeup call for an alternative idea to re-establish the lost dignity of the African people.

Considering a constitutional democracy, as a political theory, Mutunga argues that no man can be subjected to the political power of another without his own consent. Obedience to the authority is thus legitimate by voluntary submission to those who exercise authority[55]. The meaning here is that those who hold power, should do so with the consent of the people. This is embedded in the democratic values and principles. The meaning here is that the people make a contract with those who govern. Rousseau's idea of a social contact or covenant in some ways however, appear to be fraud since that it may end up serving one party to the contract and subjecting the other to a position of no rights.

In that sense, the constitution is there to serve government by empowering it and not the citizenry as the other party to the contract.

---

[53] J.Y. Mokgoro. "Ubuntu and the Law in South Africa." *Colloquium*. Potchefstroom: Konrad-Adenauer-Stiftung, 1998,4.

[54] J.Y. Mokgoro, 4.

[55] Willy, Mutunga. "Constitutions, Law and Civil Society: Discourses on the legitimacy of people's power." *In constitutionalism in Africa: Creating opportunities, facing challenges*, by J. Oloka-Onyango, Kampala: Fountain Publishers, 2001, 134.

This can be a serious problem because the powers of government are supposed to be limited by law through a written or unwritten constitution of which all those in power are obliged to obey. Otherwise, the constitution, will have no meaning.

When the constitution loses meaning, it gives birth to distorted conceptions of constitutionalism and the ideology of 'a strong man' and 'one party-rule' that have often been used by segments of society to legitimise irresponsible behaviour of leaders and to frustrate public demands for the rule of law and democracy. Uniformly, legitimacy of indigenous rule came under serious question, as misgovernment provoked social discontent and alienation of society from the state[56]. The meaning of constitutionalism is lost as traced in the words of Okoth-Ogenda that instead of controlling government, the constitution is there to serve government.

With all the cited problems, the idea of the supremacy of the constitution continues to persist and scholars like Olasunkanmi have observed that the constitution is supposed to be higher than anybody of legal regulations in human society[57]. As already pointed out by Holmes that a constitution as a supreme document, disempowers short sighted majorities with binding norms so as to limit a situation of chaos. Jubril and some others are of a view that it is difficult to do away with a constitution because it prescribes rights, responsibilities, obligations, and duties. It distributes, secures, and limits authority and powers, aggregates, and articulates aspirations and interests and outlines procedures for actions, and interactions and sanctions default[58]. All these principles can be found enshrined in a written document known as a constitution. It can therefore be argued here that although Ubuntu can promote common good but, cannot defend

[56] Akiba' Okoni. "In Search of Constitutional Order." In Constitutionalism and society in Africa, by Okoni Akiba, xi. Ohio University. Ashgate Publishing Ltd., 2004.

[57] Aborisade, Olasunkanmi. "Constitution without constitutionalism: Interrogating the Africa experience". *Arts and Humanities Open Access Journal*. (Medcrave) 2, no.5, 2018. Available at: https://medcraveonline.com/AHOAJ/constitution-without-constitutionalism-interrogating-the-africa-experience.html.

[58] B.M., Jubril. *Concept, Theory and Evolution of constitution concept constitutionalism and national Question: Centre for constitutionalism and demilitarization*, Lagos, 2000,16.

us from evil. A well-articulated law therefore is still needed. In so many ways, the law is still perceived as supreme.

Aristotle's view dating back (384 BC – 322 BC) was based on the argument that people needed the discipline of law to habituate them into doing the right thing, from which standpoint they could then appreciate why doing the right thing was the right thing to do[59]. Without a clear law, it is difficult to bring about that discipline. Aristotle's view is still accepted by law scholars in the contemporary world. In practice, if reference is made to a constitutional state, or constitutionalism, it means that if a state that displays certain characteristics, such as supremacy of the constitution (and the subordination of government to it), protection of fundamental rights, an independent judiciary, and democratic principles such as universal suffrage regular multi-party elections, and separation of powers[60]. If such principles are adherently followed, then the state is governed according to the rule of law, however the existence of a written document on its own may not be condition enough to satisfy that a state is a constitutional state. In addition to a written document, there are other important things that need to follow to the completion of the journey, to a stage, a state can now be referred to as a constitutional state.

That journey can be compared to a journey a written cheque makes to the point it is turned into cash. A written cheque the potential of being turned into cash, but when it remains a written paper and not cashed, it carries no actualised value. In this sense, it is important to understand that constitutionalism involves much more than a written document or the study of constitutional texts and structures. According to Okoni Akiba, it includes critical analysis of social forces that are rooted in a popular base[61]. This opens to the question as who the sovereign really is in the contemporary constitutional democracy. As there are so many ideas regarding the

---

[59] See Aristotle.

[60] See Rautenbach and Malherbe (2009:26-27).

[61] Akiba, Okoni. "In search of Constitutional Order. *In Constitutionalism and Society in Africa*, by Okoni Akiba. Ohio University: Ashgate Publishing Ltd., 2004,15.

sovereign, the most common one is based on popular sovereignty. "Who is the Sovereign in a Constitutional democracy?"

A Constitutional Democracy

Before looking at the definition of a constitutional democracy, it is important first to look at what is meant by the term 'majoritarian democracy' because it is a theme appearing so many times in this paper. 'Majoritarian' is a traditional political philosophy that asserts that a majority of the population is entitled to a certain degree of primacy in society and has the right to make decisions that affect the society. According to Heffernan, a majoritarian democracy places power in the hands of a majority (and often a plurality, a majority over all other minorities, but not all other minorities together, nor an overall majority) and centralises decision making[62]. Sounds good? However, there is much more to this.

Loveland cites a problem of majoritarianism and argues that as long as the reason of man continues to be fallible, and he is at liberty to exercise it, different opinions will be formed ... A zeal for different opinions concerning religion, concerning government, the unequal distribution of property......have, in turn, divided mankind into parties, inflamed them with mutual animosity, and rendered them much more disposed to vex and oppress each other than to co-operate for their common good[63]. In such a scenario, the rule of law is needed for the protection of individual rights, liberty, and property guided by the law of the land.

One of the important key aspects of a constitutional democracy is freedom of speech. However, in any constitutional democracy, men will always take different views on all manner of questions, and it is an inevitable and indispensable component of both individual and collective liberty. According to Warburton, liberty whether individual or collective have to be limited by law. Imagine a situation whereby liberty is unlimited, it would lead to social chaos in which

---

[62] Heffernan, 2005, 13.

[63] Ian, Loveland. "*Constitutional Law, Administrative Law, and Human Rights*. Sixth Edition. Oxford: Oxford University Press, 2012,10.

men's minimum needs would not be satisfied; or else the liberties of the weak would be suppressed by the strong[64].

Given that our desires conflict, it would be impossible to live in a society which imposed no limits whatsoever on what we do. It would be absurd to argue that we would all have an unlimited licence to do whatever we like no matter who is affected by actions. Having the law in place, means that one is at liberty, but that liberty must be within the constraints of the law. Democracy must not be understood in terms of chaotic majority rule, but rather as the cornerstone of the rule of law. But then, what is a constitutional democracy? Reflecting back to the term 'Constitutional Democracy', as the word appears, it is formed out of two separate words 'constitution' and then 'democracy.'

What is meant by 'democracy' in a constitutional democracy?

The word 'Democracy' is taken from the Greek word '*demos*' (people) and '*kratos*' (rule) basically means a government in which the supreme power is vested in the people. Democracy as a system of governance refers to a direct democracy whereby the people directly deliberate and decide on the legislation or through representation. A constitutional democracy therefore is defined by the existence of a constitution which may be a legal instrument or merely a set of fixed norms or principles generally accepted as the fundamental law of the polity that effectively controls the exercise of political power and it can refer to Republics like France, Kenya etc., or a constitutional monarchy like the United Kingdom, Kuwait, Morocco etc., and can as well refer federal states like the USA, Nigeria etc. According to Loveland, in modern era, federalism is a concept bearing many meanings for example as perceived by the American revolutionaries, their federal constitution would have the positive virtue of creating a multiplicity of powerful political societies within a single nation state

---

[64] Nigel, Warburton. *Arguments for Freedom*. Milton Keynes: The open University, 2003,10.

each wielding significant political powers within precisely defined geographical boundaries[65].

As already stated above, democracy started a very long time ago probably with the Greek city states. In the Greek city states like Athens, Sparta etc, government allowed citizens to vote and participate in making state decisions. The American revolutionaries, their federal constitution as perceived, would have the positive virtue of creating a multiplicity of powerful political societies within a single nation state, each wielding significant political power within precisely defined geographical boundaries as already indicated above. However, the constitution placed limits on the political autonomy of each state by granting sole responsibility for certain types of government power in the newly created national government[66]. A more general opinion holds it that a constitutional democracy means any democratic state that has a constitutional setting whether it serves the purpose or not.

The idea 'democracy' is a very controversial one, also with different meanings and keeps on changing the way it is understand by different people or actors. The way democracy is understood in Britain, may differ from the way it is understood in Uganda or Kenya for-example. Loveland gives an example in country 'A' where the law is amended to provide for a very generous scheme of unemployment benefits, which are financed by heavy income taxes on the wealthiest 30% of the population. In so doing, the law frees the poorest members of society from the threat or reality of starvation and homelessness. But it also deprives the richest citizens of a substantial slice of their income, which they had planned to spend in pursuit of their own favoured forms of happiness[67]. The 30% of the population may question the fairness and democratic nature of the decision to take away part of their income in heavy taxes and given to the 70% of the population in poverty. Some would argue that because the majority voted for it, therefore it is a democratic decision.

---

[65] Ian, Loveland. *"Constitutional Law, Administrative Law, and Human Rights."* Sixth Edition. Oxford: Oxford University Press, 2012,13.

[66] Ian, Loveland, 13.

[67] Ian, Loveland, 13.

But democracy is not only about numbers, it is also about the protection of human rights of minority groups as well.

As there are different interpretations and understanding of democracy, constitutional democracies also have some differences, but in most of them the authority of the majority is limited by legal and institutional means so that the rights of individuals and minorities are respected. But this too has problems. There are worst examples of democratic decisions that can pose serious questions for example if the UK as a democratic nation votes by 55% to 45% that all child immigrants are to be put in detention centres where it is highly possible that their mental and psychological wellbeing will be affected for the rest of their lives; it is indeed a democratic decision made by the majority of a democratic society, but with very severe consequences. Any democracy that violates individual rights or puts lives of minority groups in extreme conditions of danger, is no democracy.

'Human rights' according to Nwabueze is a concept, a device, invented by philosophers for the protection of the dignity of the human person against the growing and menacing power of the state. The human being is endowed with certain inherent attributes – the faculty to think, to believe or disbelieve, to judge between right and wrong, to feel and to act[68]. The affirmation of the value and importance of human rights relates in the main to civil rights. Political rights too, have a great value and importance, which has been greatly enhanced in our modern democratic age[69]. In modern terms, when reference is made to constitutional democracy, it has various meanings both in the narrow and wider sense.

The best way to describe democracy can be possibly done in negative terms. It can be said that a constitutional democracy is the antithesis of arbitrary rule where the people are the primary source of power in the country. They select leaders into the government, which will manage society and represent its will on the international arena. According to Hutchinson et al, the general idea of democracy is about

---

[68] Ben, Nwabueze. Constitutional Democracy in Africa. Vol. 2. Ibadan: Spectrum Books Ltd., 2003, xxi.

[69] Ben, Nwabueze, xxi.

self-government. Its basic idea is that citizens come together as political equals and decide for themselves the laws which will regulate their conduct and the institutions under which they live[70]. The people of the nation have ultimate say in who will govern them as a society. In addition to people having ultimate say, each individual citizen has liberty in that each gives purpose and moral compass to his/her own life. Each is treated as independent and self-governing as long as s/he does not violate the rights of others and s/he is sovereign over his/her own affairs. One has liberty to choose and act wisely or absurdly, but each one has a right to live his/her life the way they want.

Individual rights are best explained by the Hohfeldian Analysis whereby rights have four building blocks which are claims, duties, liberties, and no-claims. For-example if I have a right to life, then you have a duty not to kill me and if I happen to have liberty to travel wherever I want, then you have no claim to make me stay where you want. The first order of Hohfeldian rights have a secondary level of rights usually referred to as incidents and they are power, liability, immunity, and disability. It is the belief that government should operate a minimalist intervention policy where it concerns a person's individual liberties or the economy.

As envisaged, the concepts of constitutionalism' and 'constitutional states' describe a condition or state in which the law prevails as long as it complies with the requirements of justice[71]. The argument is that people have rights deriving from their common nature. What it means is that we all have the same rights since we all have the same nature. In other words, nobody gets more or fewer rights and nobody gets no right at all. In a constitutional democracy, the principle is that each independent being must be treated equally by the law and that all are subject to the same laws of justice.

In a constitutional democracy, the idea that people have ultimate say can be very problematic and most especially in the case of many majoritarian democracies in Africa. Although Constitutional and democratic theorists appear to agree among themselves that adult

---

[70] Hutchinson et al. June 2011, 48.

[71] As Rautenbach and Malherbe (2009, 26).

suffrage is an important condition for the existence of constitutional government and that elections play an important role as constitutions always have that provision as a means of democratic rule, but in line with the political reality, do not impose binding rules upon it; on the contrary, they reinforce governmental power[72]. In many of the states in question, elections are held on a regular basis but appear to be a black hole of calculated uselessness as they are just a tool used by incumbent leaders to legitimise their stay in power. When one looks critically at the idea that in a democracy, people have ultimate say, again one is faced with a problem especially in African democracies where the people are ignored, and leaders end up doing whatever they want because of the power they have emanating from the constitution.

But as a value or principle, in any constitutional democracy the citizens must be able to participate in free elections. The election process provides opportunity for the people to enact their civic responsibility in deciding who shall exercise political power on their behalf and it is a way of holding a government accountable. Constitutional democracies in Africa and everywhere in the world, are supposed to be based on a political philosophy of openness or the free marketplace of ideas, the availability of information through a free press, and free expression in all fields of human endeavour. This is so essential if people are to exercise their democratic right to critic the government. In his introduction, Nwabueze quotes the following words as in regard to the value and importance of political rights and democratic governance in general:

> The democratisation of government has, by tempering the arrogance of power, had the effect, to some extent, of bringing rulers and the ruled closer together in terms of equality. The degree of equality between the various members of society which came in the wake of popular power, the liberation of the masses of people from subjugation to the hereditary power of the aristocratic class, has brought greater fulfilment, contentment and harmony by eliminating the injustice and tyranny associated with monarchical, aristocratic and

---

[72] Loewenstein (1972, 174); Sartori (1962, 853); Murphy (1993A, 8-9); Law and Versteeg (2013, 863).

oligarchic rule and the envy and jealousy aroused by inequality in rank and privileges between the classes.....Participation creates for the individual citizen a sense of self-esteem, and a mechanism for obliging the government to take proper cognisance of importance. With authority bestowed by his vote, the individual is wooed and canvassed by a multiple of political office seekers, and thereby acquires a certain degree of importance and respect. The notion of political rights is thus brought down to the level of the exclusive prerogative of a privileged few...In Africa where the state lacks legitimacy because it originated in colonisation by means of conquest or treaties of cession obtained through undue influence, the value of popular participation in government goes beyond what is stated above; it serves also as a means of trying to legitimise the state and the form of government. A referendum to adopt or approve a constitution bestows upon it the stamp of public recognition of its suitability for the government of the community, and therefore as worthy of respect and obedience. And while popular elections are primarily a means to enable the people to choose the persons to conduct public affairs on their behalf, they are also a circumstance from which, over a period of time, public acceptance of both the form of government and the title of the state to govern may grow[73].

From the African experience, constitutions are made but then discarded or ignored. Kibet & Fombad also hold the same view when they argue that constitutions were discarded, ignored, or amended to concentrate power in the executive and weaken other institutions such as legislatures and the courts[74]. There appear to be a problem with the theory of elections by adult suffrage as a means of democratic and constitutional governance. Mutua argues that what is undeniable today is that the survival of Africa is seriously threatened by corrupt and inept political elite, unbridled military machineries, ethnic rivalries and conflicts, refuge flows, and economic misery.

---

[73] Ben, Nwabueze. *Constitutional Democracy in Africa.* Vol. 2. Ibadan: Soectrum Books Ltd., 2003, xxii.

[74] E. Kibet and L. Fombad. "Transformative constitutionalism and the adjudication of constitutional rights in Africa. African Human Rights Law Journal. Vol.17, 344.

Africa today dances on precariously on a political precipice[75]. The duties of a state as an institution under the constitution are to respect, protect, promote, and fulfil fundamental rights and freedoms to all-natural persons and legal persons. The constitution provides for accountability of government to the people of the country.

A constitutional democracy is where civil liberties and fundamental political freedoms are not only respected, but also reinforced by a political culture conducive to the thriving of democratic principles and includes the freedom of conscience and expression. In the Law teacher, Sir Ivor Jennings is quoted as saying that 'in proper sense, rule of law implies a democratic system, a constitutional government where criticism of government is not only permissible, but also a positive merit and where parties based on competing politics or interests are not only allowed but encouraged[76]. Such freedoms have value both for the healthy functioning and preservation of constitutional democracy and for the full development of the human personality. It is important to understand that for a constitutional democracy to thrive, certain values have to be held within that community such as respect to the rule of law and other democratic principles. Kant formulated the main problem of constitutionalism by arguing that the constitution of a state is based on the morals of its citizens which in turn is based on the goodness of the constitution.

As Constitutional democracies differ among themselves, constitutional monarchies also differ from an absolute monarch in which a monarch holds absolute power. The idea of absolute power is not a problem to absolute monarchs only, but a problem as well to many majoritarian democracies. A constitutional monarchy is bound to exercise its powers and authorities within limits prescribed within an established legal framework. According to the Wikipedia online, political scientist Vernon Bogdanor, paraphrasing Thomas Macaulay, identified a constitutional monarch as 'a sovereign who reigns but does not rule[77]' for-example the United Kingdom in which

---

[75] Makau Mutua, p. 308.

[76] Origin and Concept of Rule of Law. Prod. Free Law essays. Lawteacher.net, 23 July 2019.

[77] Author Unknown. Constitutional monarchy. n.d. Available at: https://en.wikipedia.org/wiki/constitutional_monarchy (accessed 03 04, 2021).

the monarchy acts as non-party political head of state under the constitution, whether written or unwritten.

But in some countries like Morocco the constitution grants substantial discretionary powers to the sovereign. Therefore, the idea of a constitutional democracy can refer to a constitutional democracy like Uganda, Kenya etc but can as well refer to constitutional monarchies like the United Kingdom, Morocco etc. The difference lies with whether the monarchy in question, is an absolute or constitutional monarchy. Heffernan points out that unitary states are where there is just one level of government, the central government, and where the powers are divided between the centre and the locality, the centre deciding what powers are exercised at the locality. While Federal states are where two or more states constitute a political unity, there are two levels of government, the centre, and the locality, the national and sub-national, and where power is shared between both by the allocation of different political responsibilities to each[78]. A constitutional monarchy is however different, and some would argue that basic human rights could sometimes be respected in a constitutional monarchy like the United Kingdom more than they can be respected in a constitutional democratic unitary Republic for-example like Uganda or Rwanda.

The protection of certain basic or fundamental rights is the primary goal of any constitutional government. The rights may be limited to life, liberty, and property, or maybe extended to include such economic and social rights as employment, health care, education etc. Documents such as the universal Declaration of Human Rights, the United Nations Convention on the Rights of the Child, and the African Charter on Human and people's rights emulate and explain these rights[79] and are foundation of freedom, justice, and peace in the world[80]. Another fundamental value or principle is that of privacy and civil society. Locke argued that human beings are free and equal and that everyone has right to wellbeing and to property, and to him these are natural rights. One very important element of

---

[78] Heffernan, 2005, 13.

[79] See UDHR, UNCRC and ACHPR.

[80] Ben, Nwabueze. *Constitutional Democracy in Africa*. Vol. 2. Ibadan: Spectrum Books Ltd., 2003, xxii.

constitutionalism is the need for the guarantee of fundamental human rights and freedoms. In Lockean thought, any positive law that violates natural law is not true law and this is an attempt to put restriction on government.

Constitutional democracies or monarchies are supposed to recognise and protect the integrity of a private and social realm comprised of family, personal, religious, and other associations, and activities. This space of uncoerced human association is the basis of a civil society free from unfair and unreasonable intrusions by government. As a value in a constitutional democracy, at least every citizen must have a right to an equal opportunity to improve their material wellbeing. The idea of economic equality is important but can as well be very controversial in constitutional democracies. The communist idea of economic equality is not the ideal of constitutional democracies. As an alternative, constitutional democracies try to eliminate gross disparities in wealth through progressive taxation and social welfare programs.

Another fundamental value or principle as already mentioned above under the Rule of Law is that of justice. Rautenbach and Malherbe are of a view that the concepts of 'constitutionalism' and 'constitutional states describe a condition or a state in which the law prevails as long as it complies with the requirements of justice. This is reinforced by the fact that generally the government and all its organs are essentially subject to the law, or that their powers are limited by law[81]. A constitutional democracy would promote and make sure that there is a fair distribution of the benefits and burdens of society, a fair and proper responses to wrongs and injuries, the use of fair procedures in the gathering of information and the making of decisions by all agencies of government and most particularly, by law enforcement agencies and courts. It is important that a constitutional democracy promotes political equality, meaning that all citizens are equally entitled to participate in the political system.

What is troubling is that the expansion of liberal democracy has slowed on the African continent just as it has globally. It is assumed that in many majoritarian democracies in Africa like Uganda, there

---

[81] Rautenbach and Malherbe (2009:26-27).

is political discrimination based on tribes or ethnicity. It is common practice for-example to have the majority of senior army officials or senior civil servants etc come from the president's tribe or ethnicity. The continent has seen many popular uprisings including military takeovers for-example in Uganda, Burkina Faso and most recently Mali. What is really troubling is that there has been yet another coup in Mali, just nine months after the last one. According to 'The Conversation', democracy, constitutionalism, and the rule of law as commonly is the case in the event of a coup, the military has disavowed every semblance of democratic tenets by suspending the constitution[82]. The continent still has autocratic leaders and some of the most enduring systems of personal rule in the world, as in the case of Uganda, Gabon, Cameroon etc. such regimes, have permitted very restricted electoral competition as it was seen in the recently concluded elections in Uganda on 14 January 2021 and opposition parties are crushed by the dominant ruling parties often using the military controlled by the incumbent.

In a constitutional democracy based on the rule of law, citizens have to be treated equally before the law. The law does not discriminate on the basis of unreasonable and unfair criteria such as gender, age, race, ethnicity, religious or political beliefs and affiliations, class, or economic status. The law applies equally to the governors and governed. Nwabueze argues that there are prevalence of certain factors working against the full realisation of the value and importance of popular participation in government. Notable among them are illiteracy, ignorance, and poverty; the non-existence or weakness of 'civil society,' the absence of tradition of respect for accountability, probity and for democratic behaviour; and massive rigging of elections[83]. In the theory of constitutional democracies, remain that the state as sovereign, is not without any limits. It is the constitution that clearly expresses what the government can and cannot do and that the state is not free to do anything it wants.

Winding up this section, at the beginning of section one, a question was posed: Does the existence of a written constitution a

---

[82] Laura, Hood. *Mali: Top 5 implications of the latest palace coup.* Online, 2 June 2021.

[83] Ben, Nwabueze. Constitutional Democracy in Africa. Vol. 2. Ibadan: Spectrum Books Ltd., 2003, xxiii.

condition enough to satisfy that a majoritarian democracy is a constitutional state? "In practice, reference is made to a constitutional state, or to constitutionalism, if a state displays certain characteristics, such as supremacy of the constitution (and the subordination of the government to it), protection of fundamental rights, an independent judiciary, and democratic principles such as universal suffrage, regular multi-party elections which are free and fair, and separation of powers"[84]. On this basis, most modern states can be regarded as constitutional states. At the beginning of this section, a question was asked: "Who is the Sovereign in a Constitutional democracy?"

In conclusion of this section, let us take for-example the extreme case of an absolute sovereign, Rex, who combines unlimited power in all three domains. Suppose it is widely acknowledged that Rex has these powers, as well as the authority to exercise them at his pleasure. The constitution of this state might then be said to contain only one rule, which grants unlimited power to Rex. He is not legally answerable for the wisdom or morality of his decrees, nor is he bound by procedures, or any other kinds of limitations or requirements, in exercising his powers. Whatever Rex decrees is constitutionally valid. When scholars talk of constitutionalism, however, they normally mean something that rules out Rex's case.

Constitutionalism in the richer sense of the term is the idea that government can/should be limited in its powers and that its authority depends on it observing these limitations. In this richer sense of the term, Rex's society has not embraced constitutionalism because the rule conferring his powers impose no constitutional limits on them. Compare a second state in which Regina has all the powers possessed by Rex except that she lacks authority to legislate on matters concerning religion. Suppose further that Regina also lacks the power to implement, or to adjudicate on the basis of, any law which exceeds the scope of her legislative competence. We have here the seeds of constitutionalism as that notion has come to be understood in western thought. In a richer sense, a constitutionalism must enduring, it must constitute a superior law, and it must be more difficult to amend than ordinary laws.

---

[84] As Rautenbach and Malherbe (2009, 26 – 27).

Thomas Hobbes and John Locke both defended the notion of constitutionally unlimited sovereignty and in it we are confronted with a lot of problems because if you have a constitutionally unlimited sovereign, it is not possible to refer to the idea of limited government let alone speak of constitutionalism. John Austin argued that the very notion of limited sovereignty is incoherent because the idea that the sovereign could be limited by law requires a sovereign who is self-binding, who commands him/her/itself. Austin argued that no one can 'command' himself, except in some figurative sense. Austin concluded that the idea of limited sovereignty is as incoherent as the idea of a square circle[85]. However, the idea of sovereignty is so important when referring to constitutional democracy because it elaborates further on the question posed above in this section: "Who is the Sovereign in a Constitutional democracy?"

The Rule of Law

Having reviewed the literature the arguments in regard with the constitution and its supremacy, the attention now is on reviewing the literature on the arguments in relation to 'who actually the sovereign is' in a constitutional democracy. Since the constitution is supreme, would it be that the rule of law is considered as the sovereign in a constitutional democracy? It is therefore important to look at the concept 'Rule of law'.

When reference is made to the rule of law, it implies the creation of laws, their enforcement, and the relationships among legal rules themselves on how they are legally regulated, so that no one including the most highly placed is above the law as already noted above with the Magna Carta. The Greeks had a word that captures much of the meaning of rule of law '*isonomia*' which means equality of laws to all manner of persons[86]. According to the Law Teacher online, the term "Rule of Law" is derived from the French phrase '*La*

---

[85] See John Locke, John Austin, and Thomas Hobbes.

[86] Stein, Robert. "Rule of Law: What does it mean?" *Minn. J. Int'l L.* University of Minnesota Law School, Vol. 18, no.2, 2009, p. 298.

Principle de Legality' (the principle of legality) which refers to a government based on principles of law and not of men[87].

In a broader sense Rule of Law means that Law is supreme and is above every individual. No individual whether if he is rich, poor, rulers or ruled etc is above law and similarly, everyone should obey it. In a narrower sense the rule of law implies that government authority may only be exercised in accordance with the written laws, which are adopted through an established procedure. The principle of rule of law is intended to be a safeguard against arbitrary actions of government authorities[88]. By arbitrary actions it is meant, a course of action or decision that is not based on reason or judgement, but on personal will or discretion without regard to rules or standards.

With the Constitution well established, and now come to be recognised as the supreme law of the land and primary source of law that is used to govern and from it, the concept rule of law also got established. However, it must be understood that the concept 'Rule of Law' is a dynamic one and difficult to define exhaustively as modern concept of law is fairly wide. In recent times, it has come to include international law and human rights.

A glance at current scholarship, as an example in 2006, Lord Thomas Bingham delivered the Sir David William lecture on the subject of the rule of law and in his address noted that the English Constitutional Reform Act of 2005 declared the rule of law to be a constitutional principal in the United Kingdom, but did not provide any definition. Lord Bingham however noted that the Law is superior, applies equally, is known and predictable, and is administered through a separation of powers[89]. This is the general understanding and does not in any way imply that the British system is perfect. Like elsewhere, the British system of governance, also has short comings and that is why more study is needed to improve our understanding and contribute to the existing knowledge.

---

[87] Origin and Concept of Rule of Law. Prod. *Free Law Essays*. Lawteacher.net, 23 July 2019.

[88] Origin and Concept of Rule of Law. Prod. *Free Law Essays*. Lawteacher.net, 23 July 2019.

[89] Thomas Bingham, Rt. Hon. Lord, House of Lords. Sixth Sir David Williams Lecture: *The Rule of Law*. Online, Nov.2006.

Throughout history, man has endeavoured to establish some form of law through custom, common law, divine law etc. Uganda for example operates a system of Common Law as opposed to Civil Law which operates in many countries. It is a kind of jungle-made, as opposed to the law in statutes. Civil Law on the other hand is characterised by codification, absence of the doctrine of precedent and the presumption of guilt in criminal cases.

One of the most distinguishing features of the Common Law system is the doctrine of precedent. It was an innovation that was developed by courts to ensure consistency in quality and uniformity in the judicial process. Precedent can generally be referred to as a judicial decision which contains an underlying principle (the Ratio Decidendi) that has force of law which subsequently either binds or is persuasive to future courts when considering similar material facts. The judges in such a system involves themselves directly with litigation and can even carry-on investigations[90]. But the central idea remains the attainment of justice by all.

According to Robert Stein, Dicey defined rule of law in three ways first as the supremacy of the law as opposed to arbitrariness or even wide discretion by governments, second as the quality of all persons before the law and thirdly principles establishing the rights of individuals developed by case law through the centuries as in the case of England[91]. In his mind, Dicey held that no man can be punishable or can be lawfully made to suffer in body or goods except for a distinct breach of the law established in the ordinary manner before the ordinary Courts of the land. One of the advantages of the rule of law is that it promotes the freedom of the judiciary.

By this as according to Loveland, Dicey's main primary concern is with protecting individual rights and liberties a more modern way of restatement of Lockean principles. This protection according to Dicey, had to be effective against both other citizens and

---

[90] Joe, Oloka-Onyango. "An Overview of the Legal System in Uganda." *Presentation at the China-Africa Legal Forum.* Makerere University: ResearchGate, 31 May 2020. 3.

[91] Robert, Stein. "Rule of law: What does it mean?" *18 Minn. J. Int'l L.* 293 (2009), 2009:298.

against the government[92]. This established the fact that law is absolutely supreme, and it excludes the existence of arbitrariness in any form[93]. The existence of law means that there are already well-established principles everyone has to follow – governors and the governed.

Secondly, Dicey argued that a government official, like every other citizen, had to find some legal justification for behaving in apparently unlawful way 'except for a distinct breach of the law.' This reinforces the conclusion that government has to operate within a framework of laws superior to the mere actions of government officials: behaviour does not become lawful simply because a government official claim so.

Thirdly that any breach of the law 'must be established in the ordinary legal manner before the ordinary Courts of the land[94].' The Courts rather than the government, must determine whether or not the law has been broken. One future of the modern definition of rule of law, is the guarantee of the freedom of the judiciary. Article Three[95] of the United States constitution as an example, establishes the judicial branch of the federal government. In this sense, the law is sovereign and stands above any government official.

Reflecting on philosophers of the Middle Ages period after the decline in the study of Greeks and Romans with emphasis placed on Religion and Faith, St. Augustine pointed out that 'what are states without justice, but robber hands enlarged' and St. Thomas Aquinas stated that 'unjust laws deserve no obedience.' In the first instance, laws are associated with justice. If obedience is accorded to the law by both the governor and the governed, it means that the law is supreme and therefore sovereign. On this basis, some would argue that the law ought to have an element of morality as the sovereign. In some ways, this is a problem and one of the arguments in current debates is the question whether prevailing morality should be made

---

[92] Ian, Loveland. *Constitutional Law, Administrative Law, and Human Rights*. Sixth Edition. Oxford. Oxford University Press, 2012, 51.

[93] Origin and Concept of Rule of Law. Prod. *Free Law Essays*. Lawteacher.net, 23 July 2019.

[94] Ian, Loveland, 51.

[95] See "The American Constitution".

into law: that is to say, whether the fact that when many people in society think of something as morally wrong, is good enough reason for there to be a law against it. Law positivists like H.L.A Hart would say 'No' because for them there is a separation of law and morals.

For legal positivists, Law is 'What is' and morality is: 'what ought to be'. These two according to them is not the same. Something being morally bad, does not make it unlawful. These arguments point to a problem of having an organised, and more acceptable law. On the other hand, if law ought to have an element of morality, the naturalists would call it a higher principle on which to judge the law. But the question here would be "What is the use of any law if it does not guard against the violation of any principle?" Some would argue that there is no point of having a law that is not moral as laws are generally based on the moral principle of a particular society. The only distinction could possibly be that positive laws regulate external human conduct whereas morality mainly regulates internal conduct. While morality is variable, laws are considered to be universal.

Reflecting back to the naturalists, they would argue that Common law if applied indiscriminately, can result into a miscarriage of justice in some situations. The courts of Chancery in England for example to remedy the effects of Common Law, came up with a body of equity laws of fairness and natural justice[96]. In Uganda, section 14 (3) of the Judicature Act states that written law, Common law, and doctrines of Equity will be applied as law in the courts of Uganda. Equity prevails over Common Law.

According to Finnis, the principles are: (i) a set of basic practical principals which indicate the basic forms of human flourishing as goods to be pursued and realised, and which are in one way or another used by everyone who considers what to do, however unsound his conclusions; and (ii) a set of basic methodological requirement of practical reasonableness which distinguish sound from unsound practical thinking and which, when all brought to bear, provide the criteria for distinguishing between acts that are reasonable-all-things considered and acts that are unreasonable -all-things-considered, i.e. between ways of acting that are morally right

---

[96] Joe, Oloka-Onyango, 31 May 2020, 5.

or morally wrong thus enabling one to formulate (iii) a set of general moral standards[97]. The idea of 'principle' is so essential in any setting of the rule of law. These principles is what makes the rule of law supreme and sovereign because everyone, has to be subject to them.

The Law teacher continues to argue that the concept of "Rule of Law" is the building block on which modern democratic society is founded. For the successful functioning of the polity, it is imperative that there is enforcement of law and of all contracts based on law. Laws are made for the welfare of the people to maintain harmony between the conflicting forces of society[98]. Therefore, the rule of Law exists when a state's constitution functions as the supreme law of the land, when the statutes enacted and enforced by the government invariably conform to the constitution. For example, the second clause of Article VI of the U.S. Constitution says ...'laws are enforced equally and impartially'[99]. The rule of law is a mechanism, process, institution, practice, or norm that supports the equality of all citizens before the law, secures a non-arbitrary form of government, and more generally use of power. This is what makes law and the rule of law work.

The rule of law requires measures to ensure adherence to the principles of supremacy of the law, equality before the law, accountability to the law, fairness in the application of the law, separation of powers, participation in decision-making, legal certainty, avoidance of arbitrariness, and procedural and legal transparency[100]. For Hayek, the function of the rule of law is to ensure that government in all its actions is bound by rules fixed and announced beforehand. Hayek like Dicey demand that all citizens must have access to an independent judiciary before which they can challenge the legality of government action. Is it the case that what the government has done accords with a pre-existing common law or statutory law?[101] The Courts only duty when deciding a case of this

---

[97] John, Finnis. *Natural Law and Natural Rights*. Oxford: Clarendon Press, 1980, 23.

[98] Origin and Concept of Rule of Law. Prod. *Free Law Essays*. Lawteacher.net, 23 July 2019.

[99] See the USA Constitution.

[100] Friedrich, A. Hayek. "The Origins of the Rule of Law." *In Constitution of Liberty*. University of Chicago Press, 1960, 162.

[101] Ian, Loveland, 2012, 57.

sort is to protect the citizen against the government. Judges are not supposed to bend rules to facilitate the government process. It is for this reason that the constitution and rule of law is important.

Any state institution clothed with power, is most likely to abuse that power if not restrained by a well-established law. This kind of situations happen on a regular basis even in what are, considered to be, well-established constitutional democracies Like the USA or the UK. When we consider some of these countries as an example, police brutality and abuse of power are awash our tv screens almost on a daily basis. Those in authority, use their power to kill people without giving them the opportunity to be presented before the courts of law. In the USA, many back people are short or killed by the police and not much has been done based on the American constitution and rule of law to stamp out the habit.

It is not only the USA, but other developed nations have on many occasions ignored the rule of law and in some situations international law and engaged in unlawful conflicts or the murder of innocent citizens in the countries affected. In terms of constitutional democracy and the rule of law within the borders of a state, I would like to point out one recent example in the UK that I have been following very closely as a Human rights student. This example is very important because it highlights the hypocrisy in consideration of the rule of law and the dispense of justice.

Most people would assume that countries like the UK although may not have a written constitution, but most likely be considered as one of the states in the world that respects the rule of law and human rights. However, since I have been following this case, the case has left me with a lot of doubt as in regard with that assumption. The case involves an immigrant who moved to the UK almost twenty years and got married to someone who is an EEA national. I will refer to him as case 'X'. I have followed this case for years and studying a course in Human Rights, has provided me a great opportunity to reflect on the case with a much better understanding.

Since the UK was part of the European Union until of recent when the UK voted to exit the European block and eventually left the EU at 23.00 GMT on 31 January 2020, all along, there was freedom of movement and working rights within the member states. But because 'X' was not an EEA national and originally from Africa, when he applied for Indefinite leave to remain as a family member of an EEA national, he was refused. He was told that he had not provided enough evidence to the Home Office and that according to them, his wife had not worked throughout the entire period in the exercise of treaty rights. But within that period, his wife had fallen pregnant, became very sick until she gave birth, and in this particular case, 'X' had the duty to support his wife and family, but the Home Office used the rule indiscriminately without careful judgement.

The Home Office insisted on deporting 'X' that meant taking him away from his family. 'X' was then given a condition by the Home Office that in order for his application to be considered, he needed to provide evidence that he had divorced his wife. Before he married his wife, he had made an application to the Home Office to marry his wife in the UK and the application was refused. He and his wife then decided to travel to Africa and have their wedding there. They had a Church wedding, and both came back to UK because it was the couple's home.

When the condition was given, Home Office had confiscated 'X's documents and 'X' was in total distress losing his wife and kids and probably losing any opportunity of ever having any contact with kids. Weighing the odds, 'X' saw no chance standing up against a very powerful institution. The need to maintain contact with his kids was overwhelming and therefore went ahead and divorced his wife to satisfy the condition. 'X' started the divorce process and was granted a 'decree nisi' (a step away from completion of the divorce process). 'X' presented the *Decree nisi* to the Home Office as had been demanded. Home Office had put the application on hold until the completion of the divorce. After receiving the 'Decree nisi' Home Office now wrote back saying that 'X's application has been refused on grounds that he had not provided a *decree absolute*. Usually there is a period of about six months when one is provided with a decree nisi before being provided with a decree absolute.

Eventually, the decree absolute came and was sent to Home Office. The Home Office after receiving the decree absolute, reverted back to the former position that 'X' prove that his 'ex' had worked throughout the entire period of five years. The matter was taken to

Court and the Court ruled in 'X's favour. Home Office was given 24 days to appeal the decision of which they did not. Even after the Court's ruling, Home office still refused to action the decision and sought for other loopholes knowing very well that 'X' is a vulnerable person who is not in position to keep challenging them indefinitely. Home office moved from the position of proof of work to completely a new position that 'X' now had to provide evidence that he has custody of any of his children.

Why this example and why is it important for this study? Case 'X' is important because it highlights the abuse of human rights, disregard of the law, the abuse or misuse of power by some individuals or powerful institutions with authority is still a problem in many constitutional democracies. Case 'X' has left me with a lot of questions and some of the questions are: (i) Should those in authority use the law inconsistently for their benefit by constantly shifting the position of the law to suit their own position? (ii) Should the law point to some form of moral value? etc. In this instance, there are many unanswered questions concerning the law and morality as well.

One may wonder what principle the law tries to achieve if it forcefully breaks someone's family, takes away his kids and wrecks the entire family? How can someone who had worked in the UK for 20 years, a family member of an EEA national, but then the vulnerability of the individual used in total disregard of the law on one hand and morality on the other, to force the individual divorce his wife. Here, force can be in different forms e.g. withholding, coercion, threats like deportation etc. The example of 'X' can be a case out of so many and the reason we study 'Philosophy of Law' and where necessary referring to such cases is of great importance in challenging the dominant rationale that majority are always right on a specific issue without making sure that the minority, weak, and disadvantaged need their rights be properly entrenched within the law and always be protected.

What is so disturbing with case 'X' is that even when 'X' sought justice from the courts of law, but a very powerful institution like the 'Home Office' chose to disregard the Court's decision and came up with new reasons and excuses to deny 'X' what he is supposed to have. The rule of law gives guidelines or puts in place a structure that can be followed so that justice is served for everyone in that society no matter how weak or vulnerable they are. The rule of law is intended to stop the strong from abusing their positions and power. The Law is therefore sovereign and above every individual and institution.

This explains why law needs to be stable and predictable. It must not keep on changing like in the example of case 'X' where strong institutions have often used the tactics of goal-shifting to deny certain people of their rights. Reflecting again on the idea of equity, which is a body of laws of fairness and natural justice and which has been kept alive in form of precedents which carry on and has been overtime recognised as a source of law, in 'X's case, the effects of Common Law which required his wife to be in work for the entire period of five years even in situations of pregnancy and childbearing used indiscriminately is a miscarriage of justice.

The example I have just provided highlights that even in well-established constitutional democracies/monarchs like the UK, USA etc. some institutions can still use their power unlawfully to disadvantage the weak and vulnerable especially if they know that they have no financial capacity to fight their cases in courts of law and this scares me as a student and as an observer because I am reminded that I am not safe from such actions of abuse and violations against norms of a civilised society.

There are so many examples of heart-breaking stories like the Windrush scandal. According to the Wikipedia online, the Windrush scandal was a 2018 British political scandal concerning people who were wrongly detained, denied legal rights, threatened with deportation, and wrongfully deported from the UK by Home Office[102]. America also provides another example of constitutional democracies in developed countries that grossly violate individual human rights and rule of law especially regarding 'Black Americans' and the greatest violation has been that of 'a right to life'. Some killings by the police have been carried out on screens and watched all around the world and some others not. But all the same, television

---

[102] See Wikipedia available at: https://en.wikipedia.org/wiki/Windrush_scandal

and the internet have reported so many of such cases. In many such cases, individuals are not given the opportunity to appear before the courts of law before their lives are taken away.

The idea behind the rule of law is to protect against arbitrary power and abuse of the same. Personal and institutional power can be asserted outside the limits of law and that puts the idea of rule of law in question as in the case of Africa as well as in developed nations like the UK, USA etc. It is also for this reason that the idea of separation of powers is so important. In case one institution has become chronically disregarding the rule of law, it can be held to account by other institutions by applying the law. Some of these problems, are forcing people to ask new questions as to whether constitutional democracies are and still able to meet with the new challenges. Constitutional crisis or disregard to the rule of law, is not only an African problem, but a problem to many nations in the world as modern constitutionalism is facing new fundamental challenges.

If one can reflect and trace the concept rule of law historically over many centuries to the Greek and Roman philosophers, Hayek points out that Aristotle for example is known to have introduced the concept of separation of powers (which will be explored further), predictability, and superiority of law as essential characteristics of a free state, government by laws and not by men and the idea that the law maker should be separated from the judge and jury[103]. But since there is a chronical move by those in authority to disregard the rule of law, it puts constitutional democracies to question. Okoni Akiba refers to a very impressive statement that 'all would be lost if the same man or the same body of principal men, exercised three powers: that of making laws, that of executing public resolutions, and that of judging the crimes or disputes of individuals[104].

Rules that give government discretionary powers make it impossible for citizens to predict the exact extent of government authority[105] and yet under the Rule of law, the rules must be well

---

[103] Friedrich, A. Hayek, 1960, 162.

[104] Akiba, Okoni. "In search of Constitutional Order. *In Constitutionalism and Society in Africa*, by Okoni Akiba. Ohio University: Ashgate Publishing Ltd., 2004, 5.

[105] Ian, Loveland, 2012, 57.

established and clear. It makes no sense under the rule of law to act and then set the rule after the action has already taken place or keep on changing the rules. If such a situation happens, it suggests that the rule of law is not supreme and not sovereign. The law in this sense can be understood in terms of a biased referee who wants a certain team to win. He will use the rules to advantage one and disadvantage the other. The idea of rule of law is that the law must be applied equally for it to work and have meaning.

For a good reason, Aquinas tried to harmonise the teachings of Greek philosophers with beliefs of the Catholic Church and reasoned that law is four-fold (i) External law (lex eternal) known only to God, (ii) Divine law (lex divina) which is part of external law revealed to men by God through the Holy Scriptures, (iii) Natural law (lex natural) part of the Divine law understood by men through reason and (iv) Human law (lex humana) or the man-made law. Aquinas further reasoned that man made law can be considered unjust if (i) it furthers the interests of the lawgiver only, (ii) exceeds the power of the lawgiver and (iii) imposes burdens unequally on the governed. Where man-made law appears to be unjust or unclear, then the other sources of law can supplement it e.g., divine law and natural law. What is important is that the law must be seen to be equal and just before all men.

In the Medieval period for-example, the role of the Church became very important in making sure that the Church restricted the monarch from becoming an absolute and a tyrant. The monarchy in this instance, considered as the sovereign, Austin clearly states that the law is a command of the sovereign. The implication here is that the law could be made or changed by the command of the sovereign rendering it unstable and therefore unpredictable. With this kind of power and authority, it is likely that the sovereign could abuse his power and authority.

However, with the presence of the church, she became the mechanism of restricting the monarch from becoming a tyrant and in it, we see the early stages of separation of powers. The separation of powers in historical and contemporary terms is very essential. Since then, monarchs have evolved from absolute, tyrannical sovereign to constitutional monarchs we see today in which the sovereign exercises authority in accordance with a written or unwritten constitution although it is acknowledged that in constitutional democracies, there are still some gaps in knowing how constitutional democracies can be made to function better.

Bearing in mind that natural law is unwritten, Barnett defines the Constitution as a body of both (or either) written or unwritten rules not only governing the exercise and distribution of state authority, but also governing the relationship between organs of state, and as well between organs of state and legal subjects[106]. It is therefore important to understand that throughout all this historical period, laws have needed to change in order to keep up with the changing and developing society. There is no society that has ever remained the same. Change is always happening and therefore, having a supreme law that is fixed and not flexible enough to allow some changes is as problematic as having a constitution that can easily be amended or changed. The idea is to have a balance between the two and retrain as well from abusing any one of the two. It is important on the basis of having a constitution that is fixed and stable enough to provide stability, but as well one that is flexible enough and not too difficult to change in case there are some changes in the polity's circumstances.

Changes can appear in so many forms for-example, during the Renaissance period, there was a rise of nationalism, and the renaissance period brought in a new dimension in the debate that instead of relying on scriptures, there was a need to look at the purpose of human life itself to extract 'Natural law principles' which led to the proposition of the 'theory of the Social Contract' spearheaded by philosophers like Rousseau, Hobbes, Locke and others.

Some of these philosophers had in mind that justice consists of keeping one's agreements. The ideas found in natural law played an important role in establishing concepts such as *"Pacta Sunt servanda"* (Agreements are to be honoured) and inspired the formation of democratic constitutions such as that of the USA,

---

[106] See, D. Markwell. *Constitutional Conventions, and the Headship of State*: Australian Experience.

France etc. incorporating fundamental human rights and the development of natural justice (*Audi Alteram Partem*). However, these institutions today are seen to be lacking as in terms of rule of law.

This section has reviewed the literature on the 'Rule of Law' and arguments have consistently maintained the importance of rule law and as the basis of a constitutional democracy. Sklar, having quoted Mcllwain, they both maintained that the rule of law would prevail in Western societies as long as governments were accountable to the people and the judges were free to exercise independent judgement[107]. This kind of value is held almost everywhere in a constitutional democracy. The problems arises when it comes to putting it in practice. However, the general belief is that the rule of law determines how power is exercised in a constitutional democracy and a key feature of democracy require adherence to the rule of law.

The idea of popular Sovereignty

Bodin argued that in every state there exists in an individual monarch a power called sovereignty (majestus). Sovereignty is a republic absolute and perpetual power. It is absolute because it is indivisible; however, it is not without any limits. Those arguing that a sovereign is not bound by the laws instituted by himself, are accommodated in a way that the sovereign remains bound by the divine law, the law of nature, and the law of nations[108]. Bodin may have had in his mind the notion of a state or monarchy. The supreme power of a state, therefore, lies in the hands of the government thus giving the authority to make and enforce laws and implement policies as well. The government can also punish any erring member of the society that breaks the law. The central idea here is the limitation of government power.

---

[107] Richard, L. Sklar. "On the Study of Constitutional Government in Africa." *In Constitutionalism and Society in Africa*, by Okoni Akiba, Aldershot: Ashgate Ltd., 2004,44.

[108] See Bodin.

Popular sovereignty is based on the idea that the authority and its government are created and sustained by the consent of the people. Morris opinions that sovereignty is not a simple idea and is rather complicated. To understand the different elements of the notion of sovereignty, it is important to keep in mind some aspects of the history of the emergency of the modern state in the sixteenth and seventeenth centuries. A "sovereign" is the unique ruler of a realm, whose sphere of authority encompasses the whole realm without overlapping of any other ruler. Initially, it was a monarch, later the state, then the people" (of a state)[109].

Beyond majority rule, the characteristics of modern liberal constitutionalism in majoritarian democracies in Africa, may find themselves in conflict with other constitutional values. There is an ongoing tension between democracy, the rule of law and authoritarian rule. Authoritarian leaders who pretend to apply constitutional democracy, use manipulation, patronage, and neopatrimonialism to keep themselves in power. Some argue that the first and most important example of popular sovereignty is the constitution itself. Those with this opinion argue that it is the constitution that gives common people power and protects their rights from an oppressive government.

The principle of popular sovereignty is problematic because there are still misunderstandings, misinterpretation, abuse, and lack of clarity of who the sovereign 'is' and often creating a constitutional crisis in majoritarian democracies in Africa. This problem is linked to the very first question posed in this study: "Who actually 'owns the constitution' or who is 'the sovereign' in a constitutional order in a constitutional democracy?" Of recent for-example, I have heard statements made about President Museveni being referred to as the father of the Ugandan State and the fountain of all honour within the state. In this misguided perception of Museveni as the sovereign, he has continued to rule Uganda for more than three decades and rumours are that he wants to establish a presidential monarchy in Uganda by making his son president when he leaves power.

---

[109] Morris, Christopher W. *The very idea of Popular Sovereignty: "We the People" considered.* Online, n.d.

President Museveni has managed to amend the 1995 Ugandan Constitution he inaugurated himself twice, in his favour, so that he can keep running for the office of the president as long as he can. Museveni was willing to go against the initial Ugandan constitution and therefore decided to remove the clauses from the constitution that may have stopped him from running for indefinite terms in office. In 2005, parliament removed presidential term limits first and legalised a multi-party-political system. Secondly, parliament amended the constitution in amendment Bill No. 15 (No. 2) Bill, 2017 to remove the age limit. Austin in his argument, fronts a theory that sovereignty may lie with the people, or some other person or body whose authority is unlimited, but all comes down to what actually happens in reality. Although Paine continued to argue that government bodies e.g., parliament or the judiciary can be limited by constitutional law, but the sovereign i.e., 'the people' remains unlimited[110]. The people therefore are the ultimate source of the authority of a constitutional democratic government which derives its rights to govern from their consent.

In the early political philosophy stages, the law was perceived as a command of the sovereign. It is on this basis that John Austin defined law as 'command of the sovereign'. Many of the African leaders see themselves in this position of the sovereign. The orders they give, is what is perceived as law because as according to Austin, 'law is a command of the sovereign. Positive law consists of those commands laid down by a sovereign (or its agents) therefore the sovereign can be defined as a person (or determinate body of persons) who receives habitual obedience from the bulk of the population.

Political philosophy has developed and moved on from the early interpretations and understanding of the king or monarchy as the sovereign and today new ideas see the people or the constitution as the sovereign. The debate continues as to who the exact sovereign is in a democratic state. There is a belief that ultimate authority is vested in the people themselves who have the power even to change the constitution. This point of view, however, does not deter those who argue for constitutional sovereignty. John Austin and Thomas

---

[110] See John Austin. The Province of Jurisprudence determined. Edited by W.E. Rumble. Cambridge: Cambridge University Press, 1995.

Hobbes on this basis articulated the command theory of law. However, our problem in the contemporary majoritarian democracies lies in properly defining who the sovereign is.

Whoever we identify with as the sovereign has in it some problems. H.L.A Hart tried to point out this paradox when he argued that if we identify the commanders with 'the people', then one has a paradoxical result whereby the commanders are commanding the commanders[111]. This means that there must be a fixed mechanism on which government must be run. In Barnett's view, there is a general theory that the constitution deals with the overall structure of the government as defined in the constitution, the relations among the branches as developed historically, and the relation between the national and state governments. It must be noted that within this same theory, there are however, different theories like conservatism and liberalism that can be explored further by academicians.

In the case of Africa where authoritarian and dictatorial regimes have been the order of the day, the question is whether the population 'as sovereign' has a right to rebel to change or overthrow a dictatorship and whether such means are both constitutional and legal. According to Mutunga the constitutionality and legality of peaceful mass action means that civil society becomes an arena of contesting political power with the capacity of capturing the state. But many civil society activists have argued that such capture of the state by the forces of civil society, must be interim[112]. Under popular sovereignty, the masses can and should exercise the role of effective checks and balances where necessary and readiness to contest for and secure political power. The problem arises when such mechanisms even if prevalent but are non-effective.

On this basis, Mutunga is of a view that the concept of popular sovereignty justifies the right of the people to overthrow tyrannical, oppressive, and despotic governments. Mutunga continues to argue that the concept has been exercised throughout history by both the bourgeoisie and the working class. The Americans used it to throw out the British in 1776, as did the French to create a republic. South

---

[111] See H.L.A. Hart. The Concept of Law. Oxford: Oxford University Press., 1994.
[112] Willy, Mutunga, 2001, 128.

Africans used it against Apartheid and Mau Mau against the British in colonial Kenya[113].

Mutunga citing Dias, paraphrases Rousseau in the following way:

> Rousseau set out to evolve a community in which the community as such would protect the individual; but which at the same time the individual would remain free from oppression. All should participate in policymaking. Accordingly…. the individuals did not surrender their rights to any single sovereign, but to society as a whole, and this is their guarantee of freedom and equality. Society having come into being for this purpose, is expected to restore these rights to its members as civil liberties….[114]

Constitutionalism is a political philosophy based on the idea that government authority is derived from the people as a characteristic of a constitutional democracy. Paine tried to stress that a constitution is not an act of government but of people constituting government, and a government without a constitution is power without a right[115]. With popular sovereignty, it can be argued that it is a principle that government gets its authority from the people. In any constitutional democracy therefore, the people are sovereign.

Comparison can now be made between figure 1 and 2 below. In figure 1, the constitution and the rule of law is accorded supremacy over all other institutions. Figure 2 illustrates the people as the sovereign based on the theory of popular sovereignty. Further in figure 1, the theories of the constitution as the supreme document and source of law are illustrated and the doctrine/theory of separation of powers.

---

[113] Mutunga, Willy, 129.

[114] Willy, Mutunga, 133.

[115] T. Paine. Rights of man, New York: Collins, 1969, 93.

Figure 2

```
                    ┌─────────────────┐
                    │     People      │
                    └─────────────────┘
                             ↕
                    ┌─────────────────┐
                    │  Constitution   │
                    └─────────────────┘
        ┌────────────────────┼────────────────────┐
        ▼                    ▼                    ▼
┌───────────────┐  ┌───────────────┐  ┌───────────────┐
│   Executive   │  │  Legislature  │  │   Judiciary   │
└───────────────┘  └───────────────┘  └───────────────┘
```

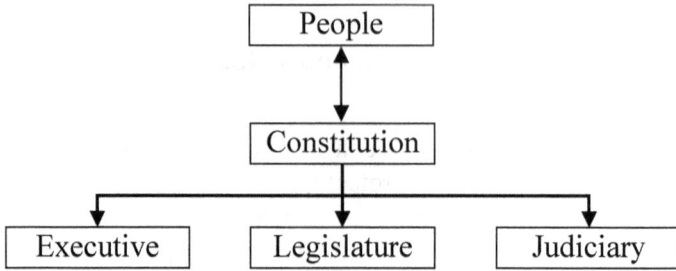

The idea that the people or the constitution are sovereign without it happening in reality, remains a fallacy and a source of woes in majoritarian democracies in Africa. Sklar in his opinion argued that Africa's major contribution to political thought and practice is what he calls 'dual majesty[116].' If leaders can amend constitutions whenever they wish in their favour in order to keep themselves and their dominant parties in power, then the begs for this question; "who actually 'owns' the Constitution or 'the sovereign' in a constitutional order in a majoritarian democracy in Africa" is very important.

In an event that the question of constitutional amendment arises, the first problem lies with what sort of amendment is being sought. If the amendment is intended: (i) to further the interests of the lawgiver only, (ii) exceeds the power of the lawgiver and (iii) imposes burdens unequally on the governed, then the people as the sovereign have to be consulted in a public vote or referendum. In case of very important and sensitive amendments, it is not up to parliament working together with the executive to make them without first consulting the public.

Those who argue for the sovereignty of the people, if the people are consulted, it puts the people in the right place as the sovereign and realists too argue along the same lines. With the theory of the people as sovereign, it creates a paradox because the people must obey the law in that case the law is sovereign. However, the law cannot command itself and therefore is created with the consent of the people either directly or indirectly. In a constitutional state, the

---

[116] Richard L. Sklar, "Democracy in Africa," African Studies Review, Vol. 26, Nos. 3&4 (1983).

people also cannot do whatever they want because they are bound by the rules of the constitution. The relationship between the people and the constitution, is so essential to understand to make a constitutional democracy work.

Thomas Harrington appears to be against the government of men as sovereigns and in favour of government of laws and for very good reasons. Modern constitutionalism borrowed from these thoughts and therefore they are so relevant when one looks at constitutional amendments intended for the benefit of incumbent leaders. It is argued that natural laws are conformed to for the good of society[117].

The very notion of limited sovereignty as argued by John Austin is incoherent because the idea that the sovereign could be limited by law requires a sovereign who is self-binding, who commands him/her/itself. Austin argued that no one can 'command' himself, except in some figurative sense. Austin concluded that the idea of limited sovereignty is as incoherent as the idea of a square circle[118]. Any limited government in the actual sense must have in place a functional constitution and other functional checks and balances limiting the power of the government in question. If there is a problem with the function ability as it is the case in many majoritarian democracies in Africa, then Austin's conclusion cannot be ruled out that the idea of limited government is incoherent.

According to Watson[119] and Lijphart[120], constitutions set the rules and powers of the governors and the rules of the political game. The constitution as the law of the land, it is accorded supremacy over and above other sources of constitutional law. If one is to choose between people's sovereignty and the rule of law, Locke favoured constitutionalism on the basis that people have a right to give themselves a constitution referring to the idea of natural rights and in

---

[117] D. Fellman. Constitutionalism. Edited by P. Wiener. Vol. 1. New York: Charles Scriber's Sons, 1979.

[118] See John Locke, John Austin, and Thomas Hobbes.

[119] "The Constitution." In Politics in Australia, by L. Watson, edited by R. Smith, 51 – 64. North Sydney: Allen & Unwin, 1989.

[120] Arend, Lijhard. Democracies; patterns of majoritarian and consensus Government in Twenty-One Countries. New Haven: Yale University Press, 1984.

favour of division of law-making power. So, in order to preserve the fundamental freedoms of the individual, and to maintain his dignity and personality, the Constitution should be permeated with 'constitutionalism'; and must have some inbuilt restrictions on the powers conferred by it on governmental organs.

The Concept of Constitutionalism

Constitutionalism has a variety of meanings; historically, it is preoccupied with the problem of power, particularly the power of those who would rule, especially when the rule might be arbitrary. Most generally, it is a complex of ideas, attitudes and patterns of behaviour elaborating the principle that the authority of government derives from and is limited by a body of fundamental law – the 'Constitution.' Up to the eighteenth century most scholars viewed constitutionalism in terms of the general system of government as laid out in written or unwritten constitution. Constitutionalism, therefore, is a broad term which extends beyond the legal document written or unwritten.

Political scientist and constitutional scholar David Fellman described constitutionalism as a concept of limited government under a higher law[121]. Mazrui is of a view that constitutionalism is a process of political rules and obligations which both governors and the governed, both kings and ordinary citizens[122] need to observe. Whenever constitutionalism is mentioned, it is regarded as a synonym of limited government seeking to prevent arbitrary government. It proclaims the desirability of the rule of law as opposed to rule by the arbitrary judgment or mere fiat of public officials[123]." According to Reynolds, constitutionalism is a form of political thought and action that seeks to prevent tyranny and guarantees the liberty and rights of individuals on which free society

---

[121] See David Fellman.

[122] Ali, A. Mazrui. *Constitutional Change and Cultural Engineering: Africa's Search for New Direction in Constitutionalism in Africa*, 2001.

[123] David Fellman. *A political Scientist and constitutional Scholar*, 1974, 491-492.

depends[124]. Scott observes that some political organizations are constitutional to the extent that they "contain institutionalized mechanisms of power control for the protection of the interests and liberties of the citizenry, including those that may be in the minority[125]."

Moore is of the opinion that constitutionalism is practiced in a country where the government is genuinely accountable to an entity or organ distinct from itself, where elections are freely held on a wide franchise and frequent intervals, where political groups are free to organise and to campaign in between as well as immediately before election with a view to presenting themselves as an alternative government, and where there are effective legal guarantees of basis civil liberties enforced by an independent judiciary[126]. The direct opposite to constitutionalism therefore is despotism. With despotism, it is meant the exercise of absolute power, especially in a cruel and oppressive way. The implication here is that there can be no claim to authority originating outside the constitution text.

Reflecting to the emergency of the modern period in the 19th. Century, in it, was seen the emergence of modern constitutionalism as we know it today as it came into being at the end of the 18th. Century and focused on the first principles of natural law, civil law, and the law of nations. The American and French revolutions constituted a decisive moment in history of constitutionalism, inaugurating a new concept and a new practice[127]. Today, it is taken for granted that every country in the world with the exception of the United Kingdom and maybe a few other states boast a written constitution on the basis of modern constitutionalism. As stated by Maru that:

> Today, constitutionalism has become as important an issue as that of good governance. In ordinary parlance, constitutionalism may be defined as a 'belief in constitutional government'... Constitutionalism can be defined as the

---

[124] N.B. Reynolds. *The Ethical Foundations of Constitutional Order: A conventionalist perspective.* Const Pol Econ. 1993, 4 (1): 79 -95.

[125] Scott (1999, 4).

[126] Michael L Moore (1985, 277 - 283). A Natural Theory of Interpretation.

[127] See M. Fioravanti, Constituzione, Bologna 1999, p. 102.

doctrine that governs the legitimacy of government action, and it implies something far more important than the idea of legality that requires official conduct to be in accordance with pre-fixed legal rules. In other words, constitutionalism checks whether the act of a government is legitimate and whether officials conduct their public duties in accordance with laws pre-fixed/ pre-determined in advance. The latter definition shows that having a constitution alone does not secure or bring about constitutionalism. Except for a few states which have unwritten constitutions, today almost all the nations/states in the world have constitutions. This does not, however, mean that all these states practice constitutionalism. That is why constitutionalism is far more important than a constitution[128].

In other words, constitutionalism is the idea that government should be limited in its powers and that its authority depends on its observation of these limitations. In constitutional law, the notion of constitutionalism is important though its specific meaning and boundaries has been open to debate. The idea of Constitutionalism has been associated with political theories of thinkers such as John Locke who contends that governments can and should be legally limited in its powers, and that its authority or legitimacy depends on its ability to observe these limitations[129]. Any government that behaves or acts in a manner that is contrary can be argued that it is not a proper constitutional state.

When one thinks of a genuine democracy, a constitution should consist of overarching arrangement to determine the political, legal, and social structures by which society is to be governed. Constitutional provisions are therefore considered to be paramount or fundamental law. In this sense, it means that the constitution is sovereign, and constitutionalism means the rule of law as in function ability. It means that not only their norms creating legislative, executive, and judicial powers, but that these norms impose significant limits on those powers. The constitution simultaneously creates, empowers, and limit the institutions that govern society.

---

[128] Maru Bazezew (2009, 358).

[129] John, Locke. *Two treaties of Government*, 1689, (Whitmore and Fenn, and C. Brown, 1821).

Constitutions generate a set of inalienable principles and more specific provisions to which future law and government activity more generally must conform. This function is commonly termed constitutionalism, and it is vital to the functioning of democracy.

Constitutionalism, therefore, is merely an allocation of power but with the idea of limited government by means of (i) Powers prescribed and (ii) Procedures prescribed. Under these circumstances, if constitutional law is inadequate, the nature of democracy and rule of law within a country is affected. The notion of the rule of law implies a judiciary sufficiently independent of the legislature and the executive to ensure that the country is governed according to the principles of the constitution and constitutional democracy exists when these rules and principles are followed consistently.

Anything recognizable as a state must have some means of constituting and specifying the limits (or lack thereof) placed upon the three basic forms of government power: legislative power (making new laws), executive power (implementing laws) and judicial power (adjudicating disputes under laws). However, it is important to understand that constitutionalism remains a flexible term. One can ask questions like: 'What are the benefits of preventing the arbitrary exercise of political power?'

The answer to the above question can possibly be found in Okoni Akiba's argument that constitutionalism becomes a living reality to the extent that these rules curb the arbitrariness of discretion and are in fact observed by the wielders of political power, and to the extent that within the forbidden zones upon which authority may not trespass there is significant room for the enjoyment of individual liberty[130]. The problem however is that in many of the majoritarian democracies in Africa, characteristics of the exercise of arbitrary political power are evident although disguised with a written document as a constitution and the notion of constitutionalism.

Based on the above, Fellman contends that "throughout the literature dealing with modern public law and the foundations of state

---

[130] Okoni Akiba. *Constitutional Government and the Future of Constitutionalism in Africa in Constitutionalism and society in Africa*, 2004, 3.

craft, the central element of the concept of constitutionalism is that in political society, government officials are not free to do anything they please in any manner they choose; they are bound to observe both the limitations on "power and the procedures" which are set out in the supreme, constitutional law of the community. It may therefore be said that the touch stone of constitutionalism is the concept of limited government under a higher law[131]." In many of the arguments seen so far, 'law' is sovereign. The theories of limited government and separation of powers are therefore very important in constitutionalism and point us in a direction that government is not the sovereign.

The Theory of limited government and separation of powers

In political philosophy, limited government is the concept of a government limited in power. This goes hand in hand with the idea of separation of powers. Separation of powers originated in the United States to define and to limit the powers of each organ of government. The emphasis on limited government shifted focus to constitutionally created institutions. They both fall under constitutionalism; however, the term constitution and constitutionalism are inter-related. The idea of constitution is as universal as it opens up a new kind of debate. According to Grimm, it is universal in the sense that it asserts that public power can only be exercised on the basis and within the framework of its provisions. It is limited to a specific territory which is demarcated from other territories by borders[132]. In constitutional law, the notion of constitutionalism is important though its specific meaning and boundaries has been and continue to be open to debate.

Constitutionalism is a political philosophy based on the idea that government is derived from the people and should be limited by the constitution that clearly expresses what the government can and cannot do. Power in a limited government is restricted through

---

[131] David Fellman. *A political Scientist and constitutional Scholar*, 1974, 491-492.

[132] Deter Grimm (2016). Constitutionalism.

delegated authorities. The idea of constitutionalism has been associated with the political theories of thinkers such as John Locke who contends that governments can and should be legally limited in its powers, and that its authority or legitimacy depends on its ability to observe these limitations[133]. Limited government is a belief that the government should have certain restrictions to protect the individual rights and civil liberties of citizens. There is no constitutionalism under absolute monarchs or absolute presidents[134]. Therefore, constitutionalism is a necessity version of limited government.

In figure 3 below, the idea of separated and shared powers in a constitutional democracy is illustrated. It is also illustrated that the separate branches work together in sharing constitutional functions with each other. The constitutional theory is again illustrated but the people and other institutions are below the three arms of power.

Figure 3

```
                    ┌──────────────────┐
                    │   Constitution   │
                    └──────────────────┘
                             │
                             ▼
                          Power
┌────────────────────────────────────────────────────────────┐
│ ┌────────────┐      ┌────────────┐      ┌────────────┐       │
│ │ Executive  │◄────►│ Legislature│◄────►│  Judiciary │       │
│ └────────────┘      └────────────┘      └────────────┘       │
└────────────────────────────────────────────────────────────┘
                             ▲
                             ▼
                    ┌──────────────────┐
                    │   The People     │
                  ┌─┴──────────────────┴─┐
                  │    Institutions      │
                  └──────────────────────┘
```

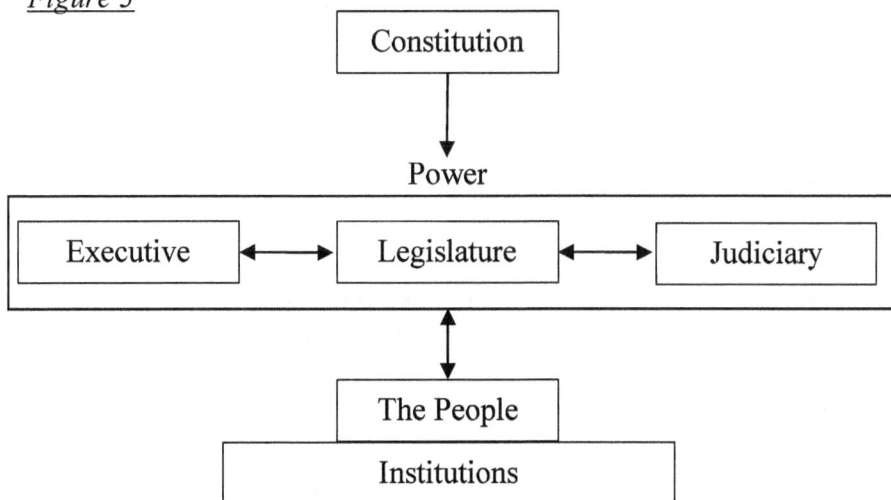

[133] Mueller, 1999, 387; Lutz, 1994, 357.

[134] Ali, A. Mazrui. "Constitutional Change and Cultural Engineering: Africa's search for New Directions." In Constitutionalism in Africa: creating opportunities, facing challenges, edited by J. Oloka-Onyango, Kampala: Fountain Publishers, 2001, P. 35

The principle of separation of power aids the government in efficient administration. The government makes a set of agreed rules which guides it in the administration of the state. Constitution, therefore, is a major characteristic of a government. John Locke argued that 'constitutionalism is where governmental functions are divided and shared, government is limited, and being limited, is restrained, and controlled for public good[135]' as represented in figure 2. In Montesquieu's political thought, separation of powers occupies a central place. Curbing the exercise of public authority, would protect the individual against his own government with respect to his legally established rights of life, liberty, and the pursuit of happiness[136]. The reason for the separation of powers is to avoid dictatorship and to bring about an accountable and effective government. Any government that violates fundamental constitutional rights could invite a rebellion.

Okoni Akiba, one of the fine African writers reasoned that constitutionalism in its formal sense means the principle that the exercise of political power shall be bounded by rules, rules which determine the validity of legislative and executive action by prescribing the procedure according to which it must be performed or by delimiting its permissible content. Constitutionalism becomes a living reality to the extent that these rules curb the arbitrariness of discretion and are in fact observed by the wielders of political power, and to the extent that within the forbidden zones upon which authority may not trespass there is significant room for the enjoyment of individual liberty[137]. Even if government would want to trespass on certain individual liberties, it must do so according to the law.

De Smith & Brazier[138] reasoned that a constitution is primarily about political authority and location of power, conferment, distribution, exercise and limitation of authority and power among the agents of a state. The constitution states and limits the powers of organs of government as well as regulates the behaviours of the

---

[135] John Locke, *The Two treatises of Government*, New York: Cambridge University Press, 1960.

[136] Okoni Akiba. *Constitutionalism and Society in Africa*, 2004, 5.

[137] Okoni Akiba, 2004, 3.

[138] Brazier, De Smith, and Rodney. *Constitutional and Administrative Law*. London and New York: Penguin Book. P. 1977, 6 -7.

citizens, be it in relation to them or to the state. Any state that has a democratic governmental system is an example of one that is constitutionally a limited government, and it implies the notion of separation of powers and the system of checks and balances.

Most constitutions, including the 1995 Uganda Constitution, recognise to some degree of separation of powers. Political scientist and constitutional scholar David Fellman described constitutionalism as a concept of limited government under a higher law[139]. It is necessary that political authority should be bound by institutions that restrict the exercise of power. The intended idea is the prevention of arbitrary exercise of political power that allows civil society to flourish.

According to Fehrenbacher, constitutionalism is a complex of ideas, attitudes, and patterns of behaviour elaborating the principle that the authority of government derives from and is limited by a body of fundamental law[140]. While 'constitution' is often defined as the 'supreme law of a country', 'constitutionalism' is a system of governance under which the power of the government is limited by the rule of law. Waluchow therefore, defines 'constitutionalism' as a 'set of rules or norms creating, structuring, and defining the limits of 'government authority[141]. The set of rules described by Waluchow are of great importance because if there happens to be any change, it should be peaceful and orderly so that the political system is not subjected to violent stresses and strains not to mention tension, opposition and to the extreme, violent conflicts between the ruling elites (leaders) and the governed (citizens). Often, leaders in Africa and especially Uganda, overlook the laid upon procedures and structures to make changes and amendments to the constitution.

In constitutionalism and in the effort to understand the idea of limited government and the separation of powers, it is so important to clearly understanding by what we mean by 'sovereign', and that can be traced in what Bodin tries to argue that sovereignty is

---

[139] See David Fellman.

[140] D, E. Fehrenbacher. *Constitutions, and constitutionalism in the slaveholding South.* 1st. Ed. University of Georgia Press, 1989, 1.

[141] See Waluchow (2018).

perpetual because it does not disappear with its holder (the sovereign). The understanding of the sovereign as the supreme ruler is limited to the existence of that sovereign. It is because of this problem that many of the African leaders see themselves as father of the nation and that without them the nation cannot exist. We know that it is a fallacy.

With so many problems most especially on the African continent and as well parts of the world concerning the sovereign and sovereignty, the concept of sovereign as supreme legislator was in the course of time evolved into the principle which gave the state supreme power. In a constitutional democracy, it is undeniable that government is an active player in people's affairs. It uses its legitimised power of coercion to determine how the members of society may live, work, and associate with each other.

In this sense, government as sovereign tries to assure certain outcomes or forms of behaviour considered desirable by those who wield political authority, and this is one of the loopholes used by politicians in majoritarian democracies in Africa to influence amendments of constitutions in their favour. In another sense, the understanding is that the supreme law supported by the rule of law should be the sovereign and this does not stop with the office holder. In Kenya for example, the Building Bridges Initiative (BBI) was set up on March 9, 2018, after President Uhuru Kenyatta and his closest competitor in 2017 presidential election, Raila Odinga, decided to shake hands and unite the country that was at the brink of war. Kenya being a better performing democracy than Uganda, according to the Kenyan High Court, the BBI was initiated in an unconstitutional manner therefore bringing the BBI referendum drive to an end. In this case, the current president together with the opposition leader Raila Ordinga were deemed of abrogating the constitution on the basis that constitutional procedural devices and laid down principles that should have been followed for any constitutional amendment or changes were not respected. The main argument of the judges in the ruling is that the President cannot initiate a referendum and IEBC does not have quorum[142]. This appears to make more sense in a constitutional democracy in reference to the rule of law.

How to limit the powers of the state is essential and a necessity in contemporary constitutional democracies as it was then during the times of the early thinkers like Aristotle, Socrates and Plato who argued that in order to have that limitation possible, then one needed to argue that there is a connection between law and morals and that law must be just and fair. In other words, there should be an element that makes law consistent. On this basis, it must be understood that law cannot be law if it is unnecessarily often amended or constantly changed to suit an individual or group of principled men. It means that law cannot function well if it is not consistent; the function ability is found in its consistence; the functionality of the law is found in its consistence. According to the early philosophers, such principles could be used as a tool to limit the powers of the sovereign in form of man-made law whether in form a constitution or other laws. In addition, must conform to those higher principles of right conduct, discoverable through reason.

The idea of limited government has been around for some time even during the times of absolute monarchs before the introduction of constitutional democracies. Political thinkers like St. Augustine and St. Thomas Aquinas in making law saw the necessity of making secular authority subsequent to the authority of the Church based on two important ways: (i) limiting the power of the state as sovereign and (ii) as check and balance of the authority of the sovereign. In natural law theory, one finds the idea that there are rational objective limits to the power of legislative rulers.

Often these limitations are in the form of civil rights against government, rights to things like free expression, association, equality, and due process of law. But constitutional limits come in a variety of forms. They concern such things as the scope of authority (e.g., in a federal system, provincial or state governments may have authority over health care and education while the federal government's jurisdiction extends to national defence and

---

[142] Unknown. *BBI Report pdf and Summary (Building Bridges Initiative, Kenya).* Prod. Kenyayote.com. online, 13 May 2021.

transportation); the mechanisms used in exercising the relevant power (e.g., procedural requirements governing the form and manner of legislation); and of course, civil rights (e.g., in a Charter or Bill of Rights). What is really important is that a constitution provides mechanism for interaction and disputes about the aims, values, and competences of institutions.

The government in a constitutional democracy, makes a set of agreed rules which guides it in the administration of the state. Fombad quoting Amissah in the famous case of attorney General v Dow said that 'a written constitution is the legislation or compact which establishes the state, allocating powers, defining relationships between such institutions and the people within the jurisdiction of the state, and between the people themselves[143].

Constitution, therefore, is a major characteristic of a constitutional democratic government. John Locke argued that constitutionalism is where governmental functions are divided and shared, government is limited, and being limited, is restrained, and controlled for public good. Any government that violates fundamental constitutional rights could invite a rebellion. Locke's constitutionalism is based on the understanding of a trust relationship between those governed and the governors[144].

It is therefore argued that there are certain institutional and procedural devices put in place to limit the powers of government. One of them, is the separation of powers among different agencies, branches, or arms of government. The principle of separation of power aids the government in efficient administration. Theoretically, in a constitutional state, government is an institution of the state and in most cases, is made up of three arms/branches with each arm of government having its primary responsibility for certain functions such as legislative, executive, and judicial functions in the exercise of power. Different agencies or branches of government have adequate power to check the powers of other branches. Checks and

---

[143] C.M. Fombad. "*Limits on the power to amend constitutions: Recent Trends in Africa and their potential impact on constitutionalism.*" World Congress of constitutional Law. Athens: Online, 11 – 15 June 2007, 31.

[144] John Locke, *The Two treatises of Government*. 1991.

balances may include the power of judicial review meaning that courts can hold power to declare actions of other branches of government to be contrary to the constitution and therefore null and void.

By limiting the scope of government and pre-committing politicians to respect certain limits, constitutions make government possible. Another modern idea is that although the scope of government power is limited, but it is always expanding. This is a very interesting idea because it means that the scope of government is not stagnant but rather, alive, growing and expanding.

The idea of Parliamentary Sovereignty

In some theories, parliament is considered as the sovereign with powers to make and amend constitutions as indicated in figure 4. John Locke argues that 'the first and fundamental positive law of all commonwealths is the establishing of the legislative power; as the first and fundamental natural law, which is to govern even the legislative itself, the preservation of society, and of every person in it'[145]. Locke argued that Legislatures are the most important organ of the state. He contends that 'the legislative power is that which has the right to direct how the force of the commonwealth shall be implored for preserving the community and members of it'[146]. Lokoti quotes 'Read' that the legislature is the law-making body (as indicated in figure 4) where government policies are discussed and assessed'[147]. According to Article 79(1) of the 1995 Uganda Constitution, Parliament is the chief law-making body in the country[148]. The institution employs a committee system where all draft legislation (Bills) must go through a staged process of enactment, including member participation and debates.

---

[145] John Locke. Two Treatises of Government. Edited by Peter Laslett. Vols. Cambridge texts in the History of Political Thought, ed. Cambridge: Cambridge University Press. P. 262.

[146] See John Locke. Two Treatises on government. 1991. P. 364.

[147] Likoti, Fako Johnson. Challenges of Constitutionalism. (No date), 215.

[148] See the 1995 Uganda Constitution.

Parliamentary Theory:

Figure 4

| Executive | ←→ | Parliament | ←→ | Judiciary |

| Constitution |

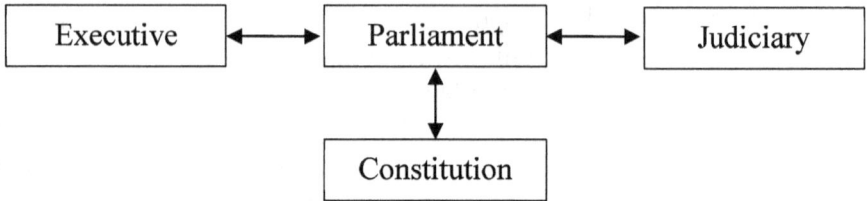

The problem is that some are of a view that parliaments to function effectively and efficiently, must operate within a constitutional framework because 'constitutions are especially important in determining the territorial distributions of power within the state'[149]. Although parliament has powers to make and amend laws, however parliament need to work within a constitutional framework meaning that the law is supreme. Although parliament can legislate, but it is still bound by the law under the constitution.

Dicey's notion of parliamentary sovereignty and the rule of law only function in the sense that he intended if the courts accept that their allegiance lies to the legislature rather than to the executive or the citizenry. But this could be misleading as Liversidge seemingly provides an example of the courts in effect giving allegiance to the executive rather than to Parliament[150]. In Uganda, the parliament is clothed with the powers to amend the constitution, however, Uganda has experienced a very big confrontation among its organs of the government whilst amending the constitution and it has created unreliable jurisprudence to the legal system. At the end of the day the issue is whether Uganda crafted the most appropriate laws and procedures that would uphold the doctrine and value of constitutionalism.

---

[149] Rod, Hauge, Martin Harrop and Shaun Breslin. *Comparative Government and Politics: An introduction*. 3rd. edition. London: Mcmillan Press. P.261.

[150] Ian, Loveland. *"Constitutional law, Administrative law, and Human Rights."* Third Edition. London. Lexis Nexis Butterworths, 2003, 76.

Johnson Likoti and David Bentham think that for power to be legitimate, it should not be based only on the three Weberian principles of traditional, legal, rational and charismatic authority, but rather 'must conform to established rules'[151]. Likoti further argues that the constitution forms the crucial aspect, of rule binding instrument. This implies that all countries are rule bound to subscribe to their constitutions, whether they like it or not. In exercising their power, states must respect constitutional rules and, therefore, not act in an arbitrary manner[152]. However, according to legal Realism it is the practise of law what is important. It is not what is written or said, but what is put in practice by legislators, judges, and executives is, 'what law is'. Law has no meaning if it remains as a written document and not as a living practical set of rules. The theory of the constitution as supreme and primary source of law is nonsensical if not put in practice.

Some theories in brief on the African context

Based on current theories regarding Africa and other majoritarian states elsewhere, some academicians like Loewenstein, Sartori, Murphy, Law and Versteeg have argued that some are façade/sham constitutions in that they exist for 'cosmetic' purposes only and in reality, have no effect. Others are in line with the political reality but do not impose binding rules upon it; on the contrary, they reinforce government powers[153]. Also, based on current studies, it is argued that some of the constitutions in majoritarian democracies are a show case and with very little meaning in terms of binding authority. This theory is very relevant as in regard with democracy and constitutionalism in majoritarian democracies in Africa.

Some constitutional scholars are beginning to doubt whether constitutionalism has been of benefit to Africans or whether it has

---

[151] Likoti, Johnson Fako. *Challenges of constitutionalism: Focus on Military Interventions in Three Countries in the 1990s.* Department of Politics and Administrative Studies. No date. Available at: https://opendocs.ids.ac.uk/opendocs/handle/20.500.12413/6392

[152] Ibid.

[153] See generally Loewenstein, 1972, 174; Sartori 1962, 853; Murphy 1993A, 8-9; Law and Versteeg 2013, 863.

become a system with fertile soils to breed authoritarian leaders and dictators. Constitutionalism has been the subject of criticism by numerous anarchist thinkers. Murray Rothbard for-example coined the term 'anarcho-capitalism', attacked constitutionalism, arguing that constitutions are incapable of restraining governments and do not protect the rights of citizens from their governments[154]. Of recent, some have coined the term "Demoncracy" meaning that democracy has become like the rule of demons obsessed with power and with very little regard to human rights.

Muhumuza gives a vivid example of Museveni and his dominant NRM party when he alleges that he and the party used bribery tactics to manipulate the democratic process in the amendment of the 1995 Constitution to lift presidential term limits. In this case, it is claimed that 223 out of 333 MPs were each given five million shillings (although the sum is contradictory) to support the amendment of Article 269. In order to maintain itself, Museveni's government has rewarded devotion with financial enrichment.

When there are no mechanisms in place to apprehend the corrupt and bring them to book, corruption abounds; thieves wantonly plunder public resources, even to the extent of "kleptocracy". "Kleptocracy" literary means "rule by thieves". Quite often the corrupt have benefited from high-level protection from prosecution. In here, we see a very good example of the "theory of elite capture" of corruption whereby public funds are biased for the benefit of a few individuals of superior social status in detriment to the welfare of the larger population. The issue is not the amount of money given, but rather if democratic principles and ethical values were compromised by the act.

Critics who want meaningful democratic change, have been harassed and purged[155]. Constitutional problems however, are not limited to African or developing countries, but extend to developed nations as well. In the case of developed constitutional democracies

---

[154] See Rothbard, Murray.

[155] William Muhumuza. *From Fundamental Change to No Change: The NRM and democratisation in Uganda* », Les Cahiers d'Afrique de l'Est / The East African Review [Online], 41 | 2009, Online since 07 May 2019, connection on 08 May 2019. URL: http://journals.openedition.org/eastafrica/578 .

like the UK, there is for example an ongoing Constitutional question regarding the independence of Scotland. The Scottish people would like the government at West Minister to grant them a vote on a second referendum for independence. However, Boris Johnson the current Prime Minister has already stated clearly that such a move will not be allowed by the West Minister government in the near foreseeable future.

The question here is: 'In a modern constitutional democracy like the UK; 'Who has the ultimate say? Is it the Prime Minister or the people of Scotland?' This is a complicated issue given the (unwritten) constitutional arrangement of the UK. The problem here is that the UK Prime Minister based on the unwritten constitutional arrangement, has first to grant the Scottish people another vote in referendum. If the Scottish people, in a democratic manner, under a devolved parliament, vote in favour of a second referendum, will the UK Prime Minister stand in the way of the will of the people and still be acting in a democratic and constitutional manner? This has the implication that constitutional questions and difficulties, are not limited in the context of African constitutional democracies. Given these circumstances, one would be tempted to agree with Murray that, constitutions have been incapable of restraining those in authority.

In regard to African countries, it is true that many African leaders have ruled their people with an iron fist with very little regard to the constitution, the rule of law, democracy, and human rights, however, one very important element of constitutionalism is the need for the guarantee of fundamental human rights and freedoms. In this context, even if some of the countries referred to have a written constitution, without guarantying the above mentioned to their citizens, their status of being democratic and constitutional states is questionable. The difficulty with the Scottish example is whether the UK Prime minister would be acting democratically or rather dictatorial and authoritatively in denying the Scottish their right on deciding on self-determination.

By the rule of law, it is argued that it refers to a principle of governance in which all persons, institutions, and entities including the state itself are accountable to the laws that are publicly broadcasted, equally enforced, and independently adjudicated, and which are consistent with international human rights, norms, and standards. Legal scholar Jeremy Waldron contends further that constitutionalism is often undemocratic basing his argument on the idea that Constitutions are not just about restraining and limiting power, but rather also about the empowerment of ordinary people in a democracy and allowing them to control the sources of law and harness the apparatus of government to their aspirations.

There is unofficial theory emerging that the legislature and judiciary are increasingly becoming rubber stamps for the executive in majoritarian democracies in Africa and playing a key role in the executive's prolonged hold on power. Uganda as the case study, provides an excellent example of this emerging theory that instead of being independent in the exercise of their constitutional powers, the legislature and Judiciary have turned into string puppets dancing on the tune of the executive.

In Montesquieu's political thought, separation of powers occupies a central place and for very good reasons. Curbing the exercise of public authority, would protect the individual against his own government with respect to his legally established rights of life, liberty, and the pursuit of happiness[156]. The function of the legislator is to oversee the actions of the political executive and not vice versa. It is argued that since in many African states, judges are appointed by the president, the judiciary may not function as an independent body, but rather to the service of the appointing body.

In a fascist regime, parliament and the judiciary are seen in the light of manipulated tools for dictators to carry out their despotic will; the judicial service is considered to serve the purpose of giving the fascist regime a technical semblance of legality in its operations; the weakest and most compromised men are appointed to key positions in the judicial service because of their willingness to bend the laws according to the dictates of the fascist regime clothed with the constitution and constitutionalism; any wo/men of integrity and professional standing found on the bench are harassed and humiliated, summarily dismissed or demoted and their amenities

---

[156] Okoni Akiba. *Constitutionalism and Society in Africa*, 2004, 5.

withdrawn to break their firmness and force them to submit to the dictates of the regime.

The problem is whether a totalitarian government can be referred to as a constitutional government. Majoritarian democracies in Africa are embroidered in a problem of being majoritarian and at the same time totalitarian in nature and this creates a problem to constitutional governance. Many of the continent's problems have been caused, not by the absence of constitutions per se, but rather the ease with which constitutional provisions were abrogated, subverted, suspended, or brazenly ignored. Uganda provides a laboratory of inordinate magnitude for a discourse on the intricacies concerning democracy and constitutional instability.

Uganda's history is replete with constitutional crises, civil wars, military coups, insurgencies, ethnic/religious/political cleavages, and violent unconstitutional regime changes all of which have caused the constitutional instability. There is continued abuse of fundamental human rights by powerful leaders in majoritarian democracies in Africa and the elections have become a useless pit of hopelessness and one wonders why African people continue and keep repeating the exercise that produces no positive results! Also, one wonders why constitutional democratic values have failed in Africa and many other developing countries.

In conclusion, it is important to note that important values and norms that bound African communities together, were abandoned or discarded. Africans had their own philosophy to life which was forcefully dismantled and quickly replaced with modern constitutionalism and rule of law. Ramose et al points out that African philosophy is the claim to the knowledge of and the truth about Africa as experienced and understood by Africans themselves[157]. It is on these lines that Nabudere states that the system around communal relationships, had developed a deep respect for human values and the recognition of the human worth based on a philosophy of humanism that was and is still far more advanced than

---

[157] M. B. Ramose, A.P.J. Roux, and M.S.S. Tsie. "Introduction to African Philosophy". *Study Guide*. University of South Africa, 2007.

that found in the European philosophic systems[158]. African people even in scarcity, had a way of pulling together resources to help one another. In the African context, the individual can only say: "I am because we are and since we are, therefore, I am." African philosophy has always been about the whole chain, the people, spirits, environment etc. It is on these lines that Okoro argues that to the African, life appears in its totality as one Great Chain of Being[159].

Andor also appear to have the same idea while quoting Mbiti that "the individual does not and cannot exist alone except corporately[160]. Liberal constitutionalism has influenced African people to discard their way of life in pursuit of constitutionalism. However, liberal constitutionalism, has not been able to be applied properly because societal values in most of Africa are communal as opposed to individualism as a value found mostly in liberal democracies. For the African, s/he owes existence to other people, including those of past generations and his contemporaries. The African belief is that whatever happens to the individual is believed to happen to the whole group, and what happens to the whole group happens to the individual. Things like protection of the environment, good neighbourliness etc, were all held in communal interest. Individualism brought by modern constitutionalism, has resulted in so many African societal values discarded.

Although African values and norms are not law 'per se', however, they go a very long way in making sure that Ubuntu philosophy that has existed for centuries have taught Africans that no one can exist without interacting with others. It is known that one of the long-standing African philosophical position is the belief that a person is a person through other people, and it is what is known as Ubuntu philosophy. In every culture and among every people, certain philosophical ideas are found, and, in most cases, such ideas are embedded deep within the culture. It may not be possible to argue

---

[158] D.W. Nabudere. *Ubuntu Philosophy: Memory and Reconciliation*. Online, No date.

[159] C. B. Okoro. *Self as a Problem in African Philosophy*. Prod. International Philosophical quarterly. Online: University of Nigeria, December 1992.

[160] C.T. Andor. "Bioethics and Challenges to its growth in Africa." *Open Journal of Philosophy 1*, no.2 (2011): 67 -75.

that some people within certain cultures have no values of their own and exist without knowledge of their own practical life.

What is the role of Legislature and Courts in Constitutional framing and changing in majoritarian democracies in Africa?

Constitutional Amendments (Change)

First, constitutions change with time, and they ought to be sufficiently flexible to allow future generations to respond to various political, economic, social, and other changes, as well as changes in the society's system of values[161]. Constitutions that do not allow for such adaptations are in peril of becoming irrelevant and eventually avoided: 'a constitution totally unsuited for changes sooner or later is doomed to become an instrument incapable of serving its purpose, bound therefore to be superseded'[162]. Second, an amendment procedure is a means to correct imperfections in the existing instrument[163]. Constitutions are made by 'men, not gods'[164] therefore even the most perfect constitution, cannot address all the society's problems. But as a country develops, areas are identified where there might be a need for some changes or upgrade.

The amendment process enables the correction of flaws or shortcomings that are revealed by time, practice, and experience, thus reflecting the fallibility of human nature[165]. Third, the amendment process assists in fulfilling people's right to alter their form of government, and by providing a peaceful method for change without recourse to a forcible revolution, it serves as 'the safety-valve to a nation'[166]. Fourth, the amendment process preserves the government's legitimacy, for an unamendable constitution

---

[161]Mueller, 1999, 387; Lutz, 1994, 357.

[162] Fusaro and Oliver, 2011, 433. See also Grimm, 2010A, 33.

[163] Levinson 1995A, 3.

[164] Pitkin (1987, 168).

[165] Lutz, 1994, 356; Fombad 2007, 31; Schwartzberg, 2009, 27, 115, 122-125.

[166] Williams, 1928, 530-536.

established in the past can hardly be regarded as manifesting the consent of the governed[167]. Lastly, the amendment process provides flexibility, and constitutions that are flexible are likely to endure through time[168]. However, the process must be conducted democratically, reflecting the will of the people, and should not be abused. Once the system is allowed to be abused by those in power, it loses its credibility.

Positive change can take place in various ways. It can occur outside of constitutional law, in the social sphere, for instance 'by gradually shifting the rank and importance of constitutional factors... and norms[169].' Constitutions may also be modified according to a procedure stipulated within them. This is the constitutional amendment procedure, by which textual changes to a constitution may occur. By the term constitutional amendment[170], I refer to formal constitutional amendments acted through the amendment procedure and not any constitutional changes[171]. Of course, important constitutional changes may also take place outside of the formal amendment process[172], for instance, through judicial interpretations or practice[173]. But all these processes must follow the rule of law and not manipulated to suit the likes of those in power.

Some have claimed, for example, that certain judicial interpretations of the U.S. Constitution are better viewed as amendments[174]. Indeed, a modification of a constitutional text's meaning may often carry a greater effect than its formal modifications[175]. Nonetheless, formal constitutional amendments

---

[167] Dellinger, 1983-1984, 386-7.

[168] Elkins, Ginsberg, and Melton, 2009, 81-103, 221.

[169] Smend, 2002, 248.

[170] Earlier constitutional literature drew a distinction between major and minor constitutional alterations, calling the former revisions and the later amendments. See Willoughbay (1921, 128), Lutz (1994, 356), I use the term amendment to describe any formal changes to the Constitution whether major or minor.

[171] See Oliver and Fusaro (2011); Contiades (2012).

[172] There is a great deal of work regarding constitutional change outside the formal amendment process. See mainly the Project of Ackerman, 1995, 63; Ackerman, 2000A.

[173] Llewellyn, 1934, 1; Strauss, 2000-2001, 1457.

[174] Coudert, 1904, 331; Levinson 1995B, 33.

[175] Grimm, 2011, 27.

remain an essential means of constitutional change[176]. According to Fombad, from the perspective of formal change, a constitution amendment can be made in accordance with the procedures laid down in the constitution. In such a case, any resulting amendment will be considered lawful. There could also be a formal constitutional change, but this will be unlawful change if it were not carried out in accordance with the correct procedures for amending the constitution or this procedure was abused.

Such extra-constitutional means may be adopted in those circumstances where the constitutional amendment procedure is too rigid and difficult to comply with[177]. The intention of amendment also has great significance in any constitutional amendment. As an example, if the constitution is amended solely to benefit an individual as an incumbent holding an important office, even if the procedures may have been followed correctly, but the process could be termed as unconstitutional because it was fraud. The table below shows Fombad's five possible ways in which a constitution can be changed.

Table 1. Types of constitutional Change

	Lawful	Unlawful
Formal change	Formal amendment Procedures	Irregular procedures or abuse of formal procedures Inaction and neglect.
Informal change	Judicial Interpretation, Unwritten Understandings, and conventions.	

In setting the 'rules of the game', the constitution must be sufficiently stable to allow participants to anticipate their acts' consequences. Fombad opinions that because of its nature and origins, a constitution will lose its value as the supreme law of the land based on the sovereign will of the people if it could be altered

---

[176] Vermeaule, 2006, 229.

[177] Charles Manga, Fombad. "Some perspectives on durability and change under African constitutions." *African constitutionalism: Present Challenges and Prospects for the future.* Pretoria: Oxford University Press and New York University School of Law, 2013, 382 – 412.

easily, casually, carelessly, by implication through acts of a few people holding leadership positions, as has been the case in most African countries[178]. An overly flexible constitution that allows frequent changes might cause instability, uncertainty, and undermine faith in the political order[179]. Second, an easy amendment process places fundamental principles and institutions at risk of being swept away by majorities momentarily fascinated with a new idea[180]. Third, an overly flexible amendment process, together with short-term political interests and the danger of qualified majorities, give rise to fears of abuse of the amendment power[181]. Fourth, a constitution that could be easily and carelessly amended might lose its authority - its value as the supreme law of the land –ultimately subverting any authentic constitutionalism[182]. Lastly, extreme constitutional flexibility is empirically associated with increased risk of constitutional demise[183].

The dilemma faced mostly by African people calls for a setting out a stark version of antipathy between constitutionalism and democratic or popular self-government, if only that will help to measure more clearly the extent to which a new and mature theory of constitutional law takes proper account of the constitutional burden of ensuring that the people are not disenfranchised by the very document that is supposed to give them their power in majoritarian democracies. It is therefore necessary to have a brief look at the two recent very controversial constitutional amendments of the 1995 Uganda constitution (i) the Constitution Amendment Act 2005 and (ii) Amendment (No. 2) Bill of 2017 as examples.

---

[178] See Charles Manga. *Limits on the Power to amend constitutions*. 2007, 32.

[179] On the requirement that law must maintain certain stability, see Fuller, 1969, 79-81. On the need for the law to be stable but not completely still see Pound, 1960, 23.

[180] Suber, 1999, 31-32.

[181] Conrad, 1970, 415; Gatmaytan, 2010, 38; Landau, 2013A, 226.

[182] Wright, 1994, 52; Fombad, 2007, 52; Elkins, Ginsberg, and Melton, 2009, 82, 100; Akzin, 1956, 337; Vermeaule, 2006, 254.

[183] Elkins, Ginsberg, and Melton, 2009, 22, 31-32, 140.

The Constitution Amendment Act, 2005

Term limits are a typical feature of a presidential system of governance in contrast to a prototypical parliamentary system in which the executive may be removed by the legislature at any time. Its origin dates to the ancient Republics. In one of the earliest definitions of democracy, Aristotle listed a key definition of democracy that 'no office should be held twice by the same person.' It has thus become a common feature of many democracies across the world. It ensures a smooth transition of government.

The Uganda Parliament amended the 1995 Constitution in 2005 to remove the presidential term limits when President Museveni was in his second and final five-year elective term. The Constitution was finally amended, and the term limits removed in 2005. There is another theory emphasized by Henkin that 'the constitution cannot be suspended, circumvented or disregarded by organs of government and that it can be amended only by procedures appropriate to change of constitutional character and that give effect to the will of the people acting in a constitutional mode[184].

It should be noted that the 1995 constitution-imposed term limits of the presidency. The debate about term limits received an almost unanimous approval. In its report, the Uganda Constitution Commission (the Odoki Commission) concluded that an overwhelming majority was in favour of limiting the term of office of the president to a two-year term of five years each. It thus included in the draft constitution article 108 (2), which provided that 'no person shall stay in office for more than two terms[185].

The considered observations of the constitutional commission and the people of Uganda were however discarded shortly after the promulgation of the constitution when a proposal to lift presidential term limits was made by the Executive in the government White Paper. Although not earlier included in its report, the lifting of

---

[184]See Dr. Bertraund G. Ramcharan, Prof. Kofi Komado and Mr. Nicholas M.L. Bova. 'The Evolving African Constitution'. International Commission of Jurists, no. 60 (1998), 12.

[185] Nicholas Opiyo, Arthur Bainomugisha and Barbara Ntambirweki, Breaking the conflict trap in Uganda Proposals for Constitutional and Legal Reforms, ACODE Policy Research Series No. 58, 2013, ACODE Kampala.

presidential term limits was subsequently included in the CRC report at the insistence of the executive[186]. In this regard, the executive calculated that given time, they will be able to overthrow the will of the people using every means available to them.

Museveni in 2003, after a meeting at National Leadership Institute-Kyankwanzi, his ruling party initiated the process to amend the Constitution to remove the two presidential term limits. Each MP was paid Shs5m 'facilitation' to consult the electorate about the amendments, without which President Museveni would not have been eligible to stand again in 2006. At the time, some senior NRM members and Cabinet ministers opposed the move to remove presidential term limit clauses from the Constitution. Many of them were subsequently sacked from Cabinet[187]. In a system where the law is not the sovereign, opportunism becomes the law, and this is very dangerous in terms of democracy and constitutionalism.

Opportunism was subsequently to form the basis of the amendment of article 105 (2) of the constitution paving way for President Museveni to contest for a third term in office in the 2006 elections. The commission observed that the danger of an indefinite election system was due to personal ambitions of leaders. The commission noted that there had been concerns about orderly transitions of governments. The recommendation of the commission was adopted by the Constituent Assembly (CA), which enacted article 105 (2) limiting the terms of the president to a two-year term of five years each[188]. As I write now, President Museveni in the recently concluded elections has just extended his time in office to a sixth term which means, he will have been at the helm as president of Uganda for forty years since 1986.

The idea of lifting term limits was not widely accepted by Ugandans. Several groups opposed this proposal. Even the

---

[186] Ibid.

[187] Daily Monitor (October 14, 2020). I regret the removal of term limits for President. Available at: https://www.monitor.co.ug/uganda/news/national/i-regret-removal-of-term-limits-for-president-chief-justice-2480632 . Accessed on: 22/01/2021.

[188] Nicholas Opiyo, Arthur Bainomugisha and Barbara Ntambirweki, Breaking the conflict trap in Uganda Proposals for Constitutional and Legal Reforms, ACODE Policy Research Series No. 58, 2013, ACODE Kampala.

chairperson of the CRC, Prof. Frederick Sempebwa, wrote a minority report opposing the lifting of the term limits. The provision on presidential term limits was amended even before President Museveni under whose incumbency, it was made, had not yet been succeeded. This matter has far-reaching repercussions for the state of constitutional stability and observance of rights in Uganda[189]. According to Kakwenza, Museveni in his own words said that 'the problem of Africa, are leaders who overstay in power'[190]. But look where Uganda is now.

Amendment Bill 2017

After amending the constitution to remove the term limits, Museveni knew very well that soon, he was going to be caught up by the age limit cap. In 2017, Museveni moved swiftly to amend the constitution and remove the age limit cap when he was due to turn 75 years old. It is claimed that the SFC (the Special Force for President Museveni) attacked Parliament when members were debating the age limit cap removal and some of them were beaten so badly that they needed hospitalisation. The observer Newspaper reported that the Mukono Municipality MP Betty Nambooze and her Mityana municipality counterpart Francis Zaake Butebi, believe that they are still alive today by the grace of God. According the Observer, speaking from their hospital beds on Monday, they said they were tortured by the gang of plain clothes security men who stormed parliament and evicted opposition MPs opposed to the removal of age limit for qualified presidential candidates'[191].

Regarding the allegations that MPs accepted bribes to support both amendments against the will of the people and in favour of the incumbent president Museveni, if it true, it is a negative implication in regard to democratic values, principles, rule of law and constitutionalism. According to the Independent Newspaper, an Act in accordance with article 261 of the Constitution Amendment Bill 2017 was enacted and first passed into a second reading by 317 for

---

[189] Ibid.

[190] Rikirabashaija, Kakwenza. *Museveni said: 'The problem of Africa are leaders who overstay in power. Global Politics Africa.* Online, September 2020.

[191] Lule, Baker Batte. *Mps Zaake, Nambooze beaten.* The Observer. Online, 4 October 2017.

and 97 votes against. All clauses in the proposed amendment were approved with minor adjustments. First, was the tenure of parliament to be extended from 5 to 7 years. The MPs approved a 7 -year term for Parliament and local government positions starting with the ongoing term as an incentive to vote in favour. This was quickly followed by the approval of article 102(b), lifting the age limit of 75 years for one to contest for presidency[192].

---

[192] The Independent (December 20, 2017). Available at: https://www.independent.co.ug/uganda-presidential-term-limits-reinstated-age-limit-lifted-7-years-mps . Accessed on 22/01/2021.

Figure 5: Amendment (No.2) Bill 2017[193]

BILLS
SUPPLEMENT No. 9   28th September, 2017.
BILLS SUPPLEMENT
to the Uganda Gazette No. 54, Volume CX, dated 28th September, 2017.
Printed by UPPC, Entebbe by Order of the Government.

Bill No. 15   *Constitution (Amendment) (No.2) Bill*   **2017**

THE CONSTITUTION (AMENDMENT) (NO. 2) BILL, 2017.

MEMORANDUM.

1. The object of the bill is to amend the Constitution of the Republic of Uganda in accordance with articles 259 and 262 of the Constitution—

   (a) to provide for the time within which to hold presidential, parliamentary and local government council elections under article 61;

   (b) to provide for eligibility requirements for a person to be elected as President or District Chairperson under articles 102(b) and 183(2)(b);

   (c) to increase the number of days within which to file and determine a presidential election petition under 104(2) and (3);

   (d) to increase the number of days within which the Electoral Commission is required to hold a fresh election where a presidential election is annulled under article 104(6); and

   (e) for related matters.

2. This amendment is further premised on the Supreme Court decision in **Amama Mbabazi Vs Yoweri Kaguta Museveni, Electoral Commission and The Attorney General in Presidential Election Petition No. 01 of 2016.**

---

[193] Ibid.

In conclusion of this chapter, the experiences under these new or revised constitutions in the last decade have exposed numerous structural and institutional weaknesses and gaps. A few of what one can consider as some of the fundamental challenges that have made present constitutions not to stand the test of time.

The recent constitutional changes, it is assumed, have failed to adequately draw inspiration from some silent lessons of Africa's dark authoritarian past. For example, little has been done to curb the temptation for leaders to seek to entrench themselves or their parties in office. As a result, the constitutional rights revolution on the continent, whilst real, remains uncertain[194]. Executive power in Africa is overwhelming partly because the leaders do not believe in constitutional rule or those provisions that limit their powers.

This chapter has looked at constitutional amendments (Change) with a focus on the constitutional amendment Act 2005 which was intended to remove the term limits cap from the 1995 Uganda Constitution, and amendment Bill 2017 intended for the removal of the 75 – years age limit. The challenge with majoritarian democracies, if the system is corrupt, a majority vote in the legislature should not be used to create less-democratic power structures or discard other constitutional values. Democracy is more than a principle of majority rule; it is the rule of law. The examples in this chapter indicate clearly that constitutional amendments are a tool used by leaders and their dominant parties to entrench themselves in power and not for the benefit of the people. The next chapter will deal with the research methodology.

---

[194] Fehrenbacher, D. E. (1989). Constitutions and constitutionalism in the Slaveholding South. 1st. Edition. University of Georgia Press.

Dilemma of Majoritarian Democracies

Introduction

The last chapter looked at the dilemma of majoritarian democracies with particular emphasis on Uganda. The next chapter will now focus on the Methodology and also give a brief outline of the major paradigms of the research namely qualitative, comparative, and theoretical methods as discussed. The research was undertaken during the period of 20 March 2021 and 20 April 2021.

The next chapter will deal with the research methodology.

Methodology

First of all, a pilot survey involving five respondents was conducted and they were asked to respond to the quality of the questionnaire and to comment on how easy or difficult they found the questionnaire to be. The method used to gather information for this paper, was mainly based on a descriptive research method to describe the phenomenon being studied aiming to look at the characteristics of the situation in Uganda. The study was conducted using also the quantitative method as the main method of collecting and analysing data and was supplemented with qualitative, comparative, and theoretical methods. The information was gathered using the cross-sectional instrument by asking closed-ended questions and interviews from different participants. In one section of the questionnaire, the Likert 5-point scale was used to collect data, and this was handy because it motivated respondents to answer questions relevant to the information needed for the study. In another section, a 3-point scale was used. The reason for the use of the Likert scale was because such presentation of a questionnaire is quite easy for respondents as they just have to tick, cycle or mark. It is also quite easy to convert to measurable data and to analyse results.

Saunders et al noted that cross-sectional study is relatively inexpensive and takes little time to conduct[195]. It is like taking a sample of water and then analyse it. If the sample is infected, it is difficult to argue that the water body from which the sample was taken is clean. If the argument is made on those lines, the sample is then alienated from the sauce of which it is part forming the whole. The results indicate what is happening with the entire water body from which the sample is taken. The people sampled in this study, are part of the Ugandan population and therefore their views cannot be entirely alienated from the entire population. Apart from the questionnaires, interviews were intended to enable me find out more on people's views on democracy, respect to the rule of law, and constitutionalism in Uganda.

Saunders et al again pointed out that the sample should be representative of the population to make sure that we generalise the findings from the research sample to the population as a whole[196]. The questionnaires were distributed to people of different categories in the population. As a technique, random sampling was used but, with the aim that the sampling was representative of the Ugandan society e.g., ordinary people, professionals like teachers, doctors, retired judges etc. The samples were selected based on their availability and according to the appointed representative's personal judgement that they were representative of the interest group. It can as well be referred to as "Purposive Sampling" whereby participants were selected subjectively by the representative.

The benefit was to collect data through the already mentioned standardised techniques, and then applying statistical methods to derive insights from it. In regard to this paper, the numbers have helped in identifying where the problems are and where interventions needed. The main goal for using quantitative research methods was to collect numerical data from a group of people, then generalise

---

[195] Mark, N.K. Saunders, Philip Lewis, and Adrian Thornhill. Research Methods for Business Students. Eighth Edition. London: Pearson, 2009.

[196] Saunders et al, 2009.

those results to a larger group of people in Uganda to explain the phenomenon being investigated. As it was going to be difficult and an impossible task to distribute questionnaires and interview the entire population, the idea of sampling then becomes handy.

Qualitative research method was used was used as a supplement based mainly on an intense study of as many features as possible of one or a small number of a phenomena. The approach sought to build understanding by depth and defining breadth holistically to refer to the 'all roundedness' of one or more phenomena. There was also concurrence that the approach sought meaning and contributed to theory development through looking at all aspects of the same phenomena to see their 'inter-relationships' and establish how 'they come together to form a whole'[197]. On that basis, this paper used a mixed methods of approach in collecting data.

As Cresswell argued that a mixed methods approach is the one in which the researcher tends to base knowledge claims on pragmatic grounds. This strategy involves collecting data either simultaneously or sequentially[198]. According to Cresswell; Tashakkori and Teddlie, mixing of quantitative and qualitative methods collects data either sequentially or simultaneously to best understand research problems[199]. According to Lincoln & Guba, they refer to such claims as paradigms, philosophical assumptions, epistemologies, and ontology[200]. On the other hand, in support of a mixed methods approach, Newman & Benz are of a view that today, the situation is less quantitative versus qualitative, and more research is being based on research practices that lie somewhere on a continuum between the two[201]. Cresswell adds to this when he says that the best that can be said is that studies tend to be more quantitative or qualitative in nature. Creswell, Tashakkori and Teddlie are of a view that the

---

[197] Holliday, 2002, Robson, 2002, Miller and Brewer, 2003. *Qualitative Research Methods.*

[198] J.W. Creswell. *Research Design: Qualitative, quantitative, and mixed methods approach.* 2nd. CA: Sage Publications, 2003.

[199] A. Tashakkori and Teddie, C. *Handbook of mixed methods in social behavioural research.* CA. Sage Publications, 2003.

[200] Lincoln, G. Guba and Yvonne, S. Competing Paradigms in Qualitative Research, Researchgate.net, 1994.

[201] I. Newman & C.R. Benz. *Qualitative – quantitative research methodology: Exploring the interactive continuum.* Carbondale: University of Illinois Press, 1998.

importance for doing mixed research is that one set of results can complement another or do discover something that would have been missed if only one method had been used.

The interest of this study is of numeric data although some non-numeric data has been included as support to numeric data which is of emphasis in this paper. Saunders et al is of a view that the sample should be representative of the population to make sure that we can generalise the findings from the research sample to the population as a whole and that the need of having a sample is very important because it would be impossible to survey the whole population[202].

In the interviews, this technique was used as well as it was impossible to interview the entire population. As already mentioned, interviews were used as a method and the procedure was guided by questions developed to that effect. The main method used in the interviews was of transcription when guiding questions were put on a paper and people responded with their views in writing. There was an intention of bringing people together in small groups but that flopped due Covid-19.

The Telephonic method was then tried, and it worked with just a few people being scared to talk with their own voices especially with some of the politically sensitive questions. In some instances, however, during the interviews, people expressed their views freely and felt not bound to the questions. The telephonic method worked only with a few people and therefore decided to abandon it and concentrate on transcript. Transcripts were then handed out randomly and on purpose based on the interest group.

The comparative as a supplementary method was used not in the traditional sense of conducting case studies of one or two foreign legal systems, but in seeking more comprehensive patterns of 'constitutional behaviour.' It thus uses a method of comparative law at a high level of abstraction[203]. As such, this research reviewed various constitutional provisions limiting amendments and analysed the rich vein of relevant jurisprudential writings and case law dealing

---

[202] Saunders et al (2009).

[203] Pfersmann (2009, 85).

with limitations on the amendment power from jurisdictions that have dealt with the issue.

The framework which contextualises the theoretical approach of this research is constitutional theory. As an endeavour to apprehend constitutionalism as a 'form of political practice' and to evaluate how such practice 'works against its own internal logic[204]' constitutional theory aims to 'identify the character of actual existing constitutional arrangements' and 'explain character of practice'[205]. The theoretical framework through which the problem of limitations on the amendment power is examined establishes the theoretical presuppositions of the subject area, i.e., the nature and scope of the amendment power[206].

Finally, Uganda was used as a case study because case study research excels at bringing us to an understanding of a complex issue or object and can extend experience or add strength to what is already known through previous research[207]. Case studies research is an empirical inquiry that investigates a contemporary phenomenon within its real-life contents; when the boundaries between phenomenon and context are not clear; and in which multiple evidence is used. Merriam et define case study as the search for the meaning and understanding, the researcher as the primary instrument of data collection and analysis[208]. The approach taken in the study is first to identify negative implications of constitutional amendments in majoritarian democracies in Africa and second to find out what measures can be taken to address the problem.

It happened that the Research was conducted during Covid - 19 pandemic. The idea sa already mentioned above, was to interview by telephone or via video call. in addition to the problems mentioned above, the method became even more complicated due to internet problems in Uganda at the time. There was also another serious

---

[204] Tierney, 2012, 2.

[205] Loughlin, 2005A, 186.

[206] Seeking to elucidate the concept of the amendment power and set its boundaries, the theory relied upon might be understood as a conceptual legal theory. Cf. Bix, 1999, 17.

[207] S.K. Soy. *The Case Study as a Research Method*s, 1997. Available at: available at http://www.sciepub.com/reference/106155.

[208] Merriam et al 2002, 178.

problem concerning data in Uganda. During the pilot study, it was found out that the internet is heavily taxed in Uganda and therefore very expensive and therefore out of reach for many. The Standard reported that Uganda's parliament has passed a controversial tax on people using social media platforms. The law imposes a 200-shilling daily levy on people using internet messaging platforms[209]. In some situations, I had to buy airtime vouchers for people I needed to interview, and I was limited by the number I could afford to buy for. Interviews were intended to be limited between 30 and 45 minutes due to the expensive internet and airtime but as already mentioned, the idea failed to work well. Based on the challenges, the idea of calling was ditched and instead concentrated on transcript interviews. The research was limited to information which is common in the public domain based on sensitive security related matters.

Ethical Stance

A brief background of the study being conducted was provided so that people could clearly understand the purpose of the research. Based on ethical stance, I asked the participants if it was okay for them to take part in answering the questionnaire and interviews. I allowed participants to choose the most convenient time for them to have the interviews and to answer the questions. In the entire process, I tried as much as possible to respect the wishes of the respondents and if they felt that they did not want to answer any question/s, they were free not to answer. Participants were asked to participate willingly and were given enough time to think whether to participate or not. No one was harassed into participating, and the privacy of those participating was considered as of paramount importance. I tried as much as possible to avoid asking questions to the best of my knowledge that could create stress or discomfort. All information provided to me by respondents, has been treated with utmost confidentiality and respect to anonymity of participants during the entire process of data reporting.

---

[209] The Standard [Online]. Uganda's parliament passes controversial tax on social media. May 31, 2018. Available at: https://www.standardmedia.co.ke/.../uganda-set-to-impose-social-media-tax. Accessed on: 23/01/2021.

Data Analysis and Findings

Introduction

The previous chapter dealt with the Methodology and the next chapter will now focus on analysing the data collected. The research has looked at factors like respect to rule of law. Can a constitutional democracy like Uganda be able to promote constitutionalism? Under constitutionalism in Uganda, whether key positions in government are contested at regular intervals and if the transfer of power is accomplished through orderly and peaceful manner? As already discussed, constitutionalism seeks to prevent arbitrary government whereby rulers govern to serve their own interests rather than those of the ruled.

In the process of reviewing the literature, it is assumed that the general understanding of the idea of constitutionalism is when a set of rules or norms are put in place creating, structuring, and defining limits of 'government authority'. Reference on this, can be made on Waluchow' s explanation as already provided in the literature review[210]. The understanding is that constitutionalism mandates a set of limitations on the exercise of governmental power. The study has therefore looked at limits and constraints on government powers as per the idea of rule of law.

But as already argued by some academicians like Loewenstein, Sartori, Murphy, Law and Versteeg that some are façade/sham constitutions in that they exist for 'cosmetic' purposes only and have no effect 'in reality'. The question would be whether such an argument can be justified given the results of the study being undertaken? Or What do the results tell us in terms of constitutionalism and rule of law in Uganda? Some others have

---

[210] See W. Waluchow.

already argued that constitutions in line with the political reality do not impose binding rules upon a government, but rather on the contrary, reinforce government powers and the conclusion reached by some scholars in current studies is that constitutions are a show case and in majoritarian democracies in Africa with very little meaning in terms of binding authority. Based on the study carried out, is the argument still valid?

Thinking in terms of modern liberal tradition, arbitrariness is identified with interference with individual rights, equal protection of law considering if it is free from discrimination based on race, ethnicity, gender, class, socio-economic status etc., and seeks to establish protections for them via the separation of powers and a judiciary protected constitution. As in the case of Uganda, is having a written constitution a condition enough to satisfy that Uganda is a constitutional state? How did the people respond to factors like as in reference to a constitutional democracy in which certain fundamental rights and freedoms are expected to be constitutionally enshrined and protected against the state?

Since constitutionalism is a commitment to the rule of law, the study has keenly looked at whether the executive, legislature, and judiciary are all regulated by law in avoidance to arbitrary exercise of power. What is the role of the legislature in constitutional amendments in Uganda aimed to favour the executive? In the light of this, the study has considered other factors like whether under the 1995 Uganda Constitution, the executive and legislature behaved in lawfully justified manner to remove the term limits from the constitution in 2005. And whether under the same constitution, the executive and legislature behaved in lawfully justified manner to remove the age limit cap from the Constitution in 2017. Since a durable constitution must have a unique blend of rigidity and flexibility, on such very important matters like the changing of the constitution in 2015 and 2017, there could have been a referendum since a constitution is a people's document and that all authority on very important constitutional matters, belongs to the people.

The study has also keenly looked at whether civil society has been given room to flourish as enshrined in the 1995 Uganda constitution. J. Lane for example argues in the literature review above that political authority should be bound by institutions that restrict the exercise of power[211]. The study has therefore considered whether each branch of government has adequate powers to check the powers of other branches of government as provided for under the current 1995 constitution. Based on the available information, it is suggested that under the rule of law, it is important that the judiciary has the independence and ability in practical terms to exercise effective checks on government. Do the Courts in Uganda play a crucial role in the protection of fundamental constitutional values, including human rights? One major problem as in the case of Uganda, it has been argued that the prevalence of corruption, has made it difficult for society to flourish and for each branch to exercise its powers to check other branches of government.

As part of constitutionalism and rule of law, the study has considered whether proper administration of Justice - civil and criminal for example if people are free and protected from arbitrary arrest, and if individuals are protected against cruel or excessive punishment. whether disputes are resolved peacefully by an independent adjudicator, regulatory enforcement, order, and security, whether the people are the ultimate source of authority of government and their sovereignty is reflected in the daily realities of the political system. They are practical and everyday situations in Uganda.

Participants – Questionnaires were sent out to 50 Participants.

Of the 50 sent out 43 were received back.

The same Number of 43 Participants gave their thoughts on the interviewed questions.

Location the study carried out: Uganda.

Data Analysis

The information was gathered using the cross-sectional instrument by asking closed-ended questions and transcript interviews questions aimed at different participants. In section 'A' of the questionnaire, the Likert 5-point scale was used to collect data,

---

[211] See J. Lane.

and this was handy because it motivated respondents to answer questions relevant to the information aimed and needed for the study. In section 'B', a 3-point scale was used. The reason the Likert scale was used because such presentation is quite easy for respondents as they just have to tick, cycle or mark and it is what happened in this case. In section 'A', respondents were asked to rate their views using a scale of 1 to 5 to determine their views on all 10 questions with: 1 = Unsatisfactory; 2 = Poor; 3 = Adequate; 4 = Good; 5 = Excellent. However, (0 = Not answered), was introduced later to represent questions that were not answered or left blank. For every question, the number ticked or marked by a respondent was manually entered into the table section by section. After all numbers were entered, I counted out of the 43 respondents ticked 1, 2, 3, 4 & 5 and then, depending on the number, a percentage was manually calculated. The same method was used in section 'B' only that section 'B' had numbers 1,2 &3. All the data was manually entered, and no computer aided software was used. If I wanted to see how respondents answered questions relating to the rule of law or human rights etc, it was then possible for me to group those questions and work out the percentage on all questions relating to that particular area (See as an example table 2.b human Rights under rule of law).

On the part of the interviews, the main method used was of transcription when guiding questions were put on a paper and people responded with their views in writing. The main views or ideas were put in a table (see section table 3 section C: interview deliberations).

Section A: General Data Sample Coding

On question 1 regarding respect to the rule of law in Uganda, respondents rated the respect to rule of law in Uganda as following: 58.14% of the respondents rated rule of law in Uganda as unsatisfactory, 32.56% as Poor and 9.3% as adequate. Those who rated the rule of law in Uganda as unsatisfactory when added together with those who rated rule of law in question 1 as poor, the total is 90.7%. Only 9.3% rated the rule of law in Uganda as adequate and none of the respondents gave the rating of 'Good' or 'Excellent' and that accounts for 0%. See table 2 (a) below.

On question 2 regarding the protection of law in Uganda, in consideration whether it is free from discrimination on race, ethnicity, gender, class, socio-economic status etc. 39.53% rated it as unsatisfactory, 41.9% as poor, 13.95% as Adequate, 2.33% rated it as 'Good'. Adding those who rated it as unsatisfactory together with those who rated it poor, the total is 81.43% of the respondents. None of the respondents rated the protection of law in Uganda as 'Excellent' and that accounts for 0% of the total number of respondents. 2.33% of the respondents did not answer this question. See table 2 (a) below.

On question 3 regarding limits on the powers of government which elected officials must obey; 34.88% rated it as unsatisfactory, 53.49% as poor, 6.98% rated it as adequate, 2.33% gave a good rating. Those who rated it as unsatisfactory when added to those who rated it as poor, the total is 88.37% of the respondents. None of the respondents rated it as 'Excellent' and that also accounts to 0% of the total number respondents. 4.65% of the respondents did not answer this question. See table 2 (a) below.

On question 4 regarding the idea that each arm or branch of government has adequate power to check the powers of other branches, 41.86% rated it as unsatisfactory, 51.16% rated it as poor. Those who rated it as unsatisfactory added to those who rated it as poor make up a total of 93.02% of the total number of respondents. Only 4.65% of the respondents gave the rating as adequate. None of the respondents gave the rating 'Good' or 'Excellent' and that accounts for 0% of all the respondents. 2.33% of the respondents, did not answer this question. See table 2 (a) below.

On question 5 regarding democratic values in Uganda, 41.86% rated it as unsatisfactory, 51.16% as poor. Putting together those who rated it as unsatisfactory and those who rated it as poor, the total is 93.02% of all respondents. 4.65% of the respondents gave adequate rating, only 6.98% gave 'good' rating. None of the respondents gave 'Excellent' rating and that accounts for 0% of all respondents. The question was answered by all the respondents. See table 2 (a) below.

On question 6 regarding the administration of Justice in Uganda, 25.58% rated it as unsatisfactory, 53.49% as poor. Putting together those who rated it as unsatisfactory and those who rated it as poor, the total is 79.07% of all respondents. 18.6% of the respondents gave adequate rating, only 2.33% gave 'good' rating. None of the respondents gave 'Good' or 'Excellent' rating and that accounts for 0% of all respondents. The question was answered by all the respondents. See table 2 (a) below.

On question 7 regarding the way Individuals are protected against cruel or excessive punishment, 37.21% rated it as unsatisfactory, 53.49% as poor. Again, if we put together those who rated it as unsatisfactory and those who rated it as poor, the total is 90.7% of all respondents. Only 6.98% of the respondents gave adequate rating. None of the respondents gave 'Good' or 'Excellent' rating and that accounts for 0% of all respondents. 4.65% of the respondents did not answer this question. See table 2 (a) below.

On question 8 regarding the record of Human Rights in Uganda, 53.49% rated it as unsatisfactory, and 41.86% as poor. Putting together those who rated it as unsatisfactory and those as poor, the total is 95.35%. Only 2.33% gave adequate rating, again only 2.33 gave 'Good' rating. None of the respondents gave 'Excellent' rating and that accounts for 0%. The question was answered by all respondents. See table 2 (a) below.

On question 9 regarding the way people feel individual rights to life, liberty, and protection of property are guaranteed by the due process of the law, 51.16% rated it as unsatisfactory, 30.23% as poor. Adding those who rated it as unsatisfactory to those who rated it as poor, the total is 81.39%. Only 2.33% gave adequate rating and the same 2.33% gave 'Good' rating. None gave 'Excellent' rating and that accounts for 0%. All respondents answered the question. See table 1 (a) below.

On question 10 regarding the right to peaceful assembly free of restrictions, except those necessary for the protection of the rights and freedoms of others; 53.49% rated it as unsatisfactory, 41.86% rated it as poor. If those who rated it as unsatisfactory are added to those who rated it as poor, the total 95.35%. Only 2.33% gave adequate rating and again the same 2.33% gave 'Good' rating. None of the respondents gave 'Excellent' rating and that accounts for 0%. The question was answered by all respondents. See table 2 (a) below.

Table 2 below, shows how people responded to the questions in section A

Table 2 (a): Section 'A' General Sample data coding

Respondents	Questions										Respondents	Questions									
	1	2	3	4	5	6	7	8	9	10		1	2	3	4	5	6	7	8	9	10
1	3	1	2	2	1	3	2	3	2	2	23	1	1	2	1	1	2	2	2	1	2
2	1	3	1	1	3	1	1	1	3	2	24	1	2	2	1	1	2	2	2	1	2
3	1	2	2	2	1	2	2	2	1	2	25	3	4	4	3	4	4	2	4	3	4
4	1	1	1	1	1	1	1	1	1	1	26	1	2	1	1	2	1	1	1	2	1
5	1	1	1	1	1	2	2	2	2	2	27	2	3	3	1	2	3	0	2	4	2
6	1	1	1	2	2	2	2	1	1	2	28	2	1	1	2	1	2	2	1	2	1
7	1	2	2	0	2	2	0	1	1	1	29	2	2	0	1	2	3	2	2	2	2
8	2	3	2	1	2	2	1	1	1	1	30	1	1	2	1	1	2	2	1	2	1
9	3	2	2	2	4	3	1	2	2	1	31	1	2	2	2	1	2	1	1	2	2
10	2	2	2	2	3	3	3	2	3	1	32	2	2	2	2	2	2	2	2	2	2
11	2	2	2	1	2	2	1	1	2	1	33	1	1	2	2	2	2	2	1	2	1
12	2	2	1	2	2	1	1	1	1	2	34	1	1	1	2	2	2	1	1	1	1
13	1	1	2	2	1	2	2	1	1	2	35	1	2	2	2	2	1	2	2	3	2
14	2	2	1	2	1	3	1	1	2	2	36	1	2	2	2	2	2	2	2	1	1
15	2	3	2	2	3	1	1	2	1	1	37	1	1	1	1	1	1	1	1	1	1
16	1	2	2	3	1	1	1	1	1	1	38	1	1	2	2	2	2	2	2	3	2
17	2	0	0	2	1	3	1	2	3	2	39	1	2	2	2	2	2	2	2	1	1
18	1	2	2	2	1	2	2	2	1	3	40	2	3	2	2	2	1	3	2	3	2
19	1	1	1	1	1	1	1	1	1	1	41	1	1	1	1	2	2	1	1	1	1
20	1	1	1	1	1	1	2	1	1	1	42	1	1	2	2	2	2	2	1	1	1
21	3	3	3	3	3	2	2	1	1	2	43	2	1	1	2	4	1	2	1	1	1
22	2	2	1	1	2	2	2	2	2	1											

Analysis on Constitutionalism and rule of law section 'A'

In Section A, all the 10 questions have a relationship with the idea of Constitutionalism and rule of law. According to the data received, table 2 (b) below highlights in percentages those rated the idea of constitutionalism in Uganda as unsatisfactory and poor.

The hypothesis was based on the presumption that constitutional amendments intended for the benefit of incumbent leaders in majoritarian democracies in Africa have serious negative implications. Thinking in terms of Uganda, respondents were of a view that constitutions in Uganda have not been able to prevent Ugandan Presidents from exploiting their powers and therefore the state's constitution is not respected as a power in itself. Respondents argued that soon after Uganda's independence, in 1966, Milton Obote suspended the then Uganda Constitution and replaced it with his own.

Question 1 section 'B' when respondents were asked whether they would agree that the people are the ultimate source of authority

119

of the government and their sovereignty is reflected in the daily realities of the political system in Uganda; 48.84% did not agree, 37.21% agreed while 11.63 % did not know. Those who did not agree form most of the respondents. On the question regarding democratic values in Uganda, question 5 section 'A'. 41.86% rated democratic values in Uganda as unsatisfactory, and 51.16% as poor. Those who rated democratic values in Uganda as unsatisfactory are added with those who gave a poor, the total is 93.02%. Only 4.65% of respondents rated it as adequate, and only 6.98% gave 'good' rating. None of the respondents gave 'Excellent' rating.

Based on the data, it is evident that the majority of respondents think that elections in Uganda are not free and fair and marred with a lot of violence. Respondents in question 4 section 'B' when asked whether they agree that Key positions in government are contested at regular intervals in Uganda; 53.49% did not agree, 25.58% Agreed, and 20.93% did not know. The understanding here is not whether there are no regular elections in Uganda but rather whether those elections have any meaning at all.

Question 2 section 'B' when the respondents were asked on whether they think that the executive and legislature behaved in a lawfully justified manner to remove the term limits from the constitution in 2005; 86.05% of all respondents did not agree, only 6.98% agreed, and only 6.98% did not know. In question 3 section 'B' again as an example, respondents were asked whether under the 1995 Uganda Constitution, the executive and legislature behaved in a lawfully justified manner to remove the age limit cap from the Constitution in 2017; 86.05% did not agree, 6.98% Agreed and 6.98% did not know whether the executive and legislature behaved in a lawfully justified manner to remove the age limit cap from the Constitution.

Question 2 section 'A' again as an example, when respondents were asked whether they think that there is equal protection of law in Uganda, in consideration whether it is free from discrimination on race, ethnicity, gender, class, socio-economic status etc. 39.53% rated it as unsatisfactory, 41.9% as poor. If those who rated it as unsatisfactory are added to those who rated it as poor, the total is

81.43% of the respondents. Only 13.95% as Adequate, and only 2.33% rated it as 'Good' and none rated it as 'Excellent'.

If consideration is made on how respondents reacted on questions regarding Human Rights in Uganda, as an example, I have taken six random respondents as a sample to represent the reaction and the sample is shown in table 2 (b) below.

Human Rights Under Rule of Law Section 'A' and 'B' Coding Sample:

Table 2 (b): Human Rights under rule of law Section 'A' and 'B' Coding Sample

Respondents	Questions										
	A						B				
1	2	6	7	8	9	10	6	7	8	9	10
2	1	3	2	3	2	2	2	2	2	1	1
3	3	1	1	1	3	2	1	1	1	1	1
4	2	2	2	2	1	2	1	1	1	1	1
5	1	1	1	1	1	1	1	1	1	1	1
6	1	2	2	2	2	2	1	1	1	1	1

In section 'A' question 2 as an example refers to Human rights, out of 6 sampling, [3] rated 'unsatisfactory' and that is 50% of that sample. [2] rated Poor and that accounts to 33.33% of the sample. [1] rated as 'Adequate' and that is 16.67% of the sample. None rated question 2 out of the sample as 'Good' or 'Excellent' and that accounts to 0%. Question 6 in the same section, [2] rated it as 'unsatisfactory' that is 33.33% of the sample; [2] rated it as poor and that accounts to 33.33% of the sample; [1] rated it as 'adequate and that accounts to 16.67% of the sample. Again, none rated it as 'Good' or 'Excellent' and that accounts to 0%. Etc. let us take for example question 2, 50% rated it as unsatisfactory and 33.33% as poor. Only 16.67% rated it as 'Adequate and none rated it as 'Good' or 'Excellent' and that trend goes on.

Table 2 (C) below, summarises all information in Section A, in percentages.

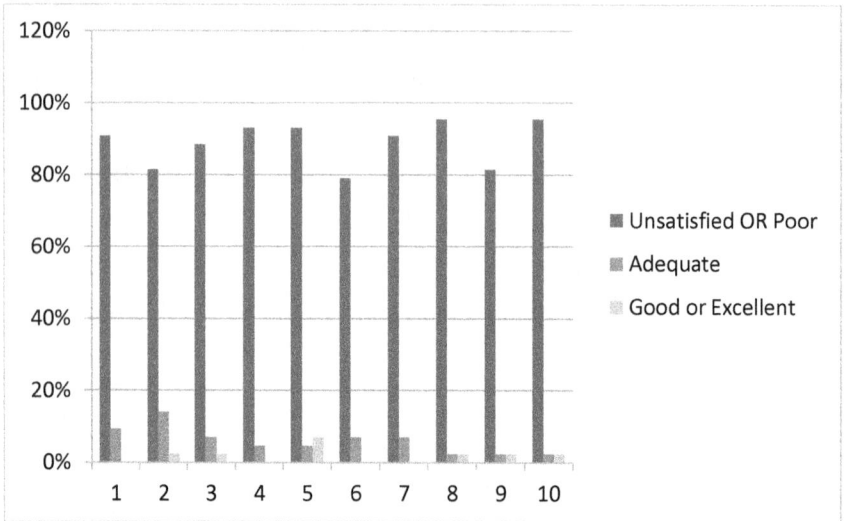

In section 'B' question 6 [4] rated it as unsatisfactory and that accounts to 66.67%; [1] as poor and that accounts to 16.67% of the sample; None rated it as 'Adequate', 'Good' or 'Excellent'; Question 7 & 8 exactly the same figures as in question 6. Question 9 & 10 the sample of 6 taken, all rated both as unsatisfactory. None rated it as poor, adequate, good, or excellent. The trend in section 'B' in regard to human rights in Uganda is very clear. If we choose question 7 at random from table 1 (b) and we want to see how all the 43 respondents reacted on issues regarding human rights in Uganda, 76.74% did not agree that individuals are free and protected from arbitrary arrest in Uganda. Only 9.3 % of all respondents agree that individuals are free and protected.

The way respondents reacted on the rule of law in Uganda, in question 1 section 'A', 58.14% of the respondents rated rule of law in Uganda as unsatisfactory, 32.56% as Poor and only 9.3% as adequate and none as 'Excellent'. Those who rated the rule of law as unsatisfactory when added together with those who rated it as poor, the total is 90.7% of all respondents.

In support of the above, according to the Monitor Newspaper published on 6 November 2020, it is stated that 'four years on this day, the UPDF and the Police attacked the Rwenzururu royal palace in Kasese, resulting in the death of over 200 people mainly women and children. Four years down the road, the families of the slain remain silently waiting for answers and accountability. Some fear to take legal action in fear being singled out by the regime'[212]. Much as Uganda has a constitution, it is limited in its applicability and has to be supplemented by other societal values and norms. But since they too have been disregarded and discarded, it leaves a society embedded in lawlessness with no societal values and norms. On the administration of justice in Uganda, in question 6 section 'A' 25.58% rated it as unsatisfactory, 53.49% as poor. Putting together those who rated it as unsatisfactory and poor, the total is 79.07% of all respondents. Only 18.6% of the respondents gave adequate rating, and only 2.33% gave 'good' rating. None of the respondents gave 'Excellent' rating.

When it comes to the idea that constitutions regulate and define the distribution of public power among the various institutions of state, whether central, regional, or local, in question 4 section 'A' regarding the idea that each arm or branch of government has adequate power to check the powers of other branches, 44.86% rated it as unsatisfactory, 51.16% as poor. Those who rated it as unsatisfactory added to those who rated it as poor make up a total of 93.02% of the respondents. Only 4.65% of the respondents gave the rating as adequate. None of the respondents gave the rating 'Good' or 'Excellent' and that accounts for 0% of all the respondents.

If we look further on the limits of governmental authority, in question 3 section 'A', 34.88% rated it as unsatisfactory, 53.49% as poor. Those who rated it as unsatisfactory when added to those who rated it as poor, the total is 88.37% of the respondents. 6.98% rated it as adequate. Only 2.33% of all respondents gave a 'Good' rating. Again, none of the respondents rated it 'Excellent' and that also accounts to 0% of the total number respondents.

---

[212] Emmanuel, Busingye. *Kasese killings: Today marks 4 years as families still wait in pain.* Online: Monitor Newspaper, 6 November 2020.

In general terms, the data in Section 'A' for example all the 10 questions are related to the idea of constitutionalism and rule of law. However, according to the feedback, respondents rated the questions from 79% to 95% as unsatisfactory and poor when added together. The ideas expressed in the same questions were rated as adequate by only 2% to around 9% by respondents. If those who rated the Constitution or idea of constitutionalism in Uganda based on all the 10 questions as 'Good' or 'Excellent' are added together, the range is from 0% to roughly around 6% of all respondents put together. See tables 2 c, d, & e below.

In the interview section 'C', it was pointed out as an example that, when the people were consulted for their views during the process of the 1995 Constitutional making in Uganda, the majority overwhelming supported the idea of federalism as a system of government favoured. The idea behind supporting a federal system was based on the ideas of power sharing and the avoidance of the danger of too much centralised power in the hands of the president or office of the president. Based on the data in the available literature, according to the Odoki Commission findings, sixty-five (65%) of all the people of Uganda and ninety-seven (97%) of the people of Buganda wanted a federal system of government[213]. However, the views of the people were ignored.

The Federal system of government was intended to trim the powers of the president and the Central government so as to decentralise some of the powers to local government and regions that make up Uganda. Because the government perceived the views of the people as a threat to its powers, the draft or final form of the Constitution was never made available to the people until it was debated on and passed by the then sitting parliament.

When it comes to the analysis of 'Rule of Law' in a constitutional democracy like Uganda, according to the research conducted, respondents believe that power is too much centralised in the hands of the president in this case (President Museveni). It appears to many as if President Museveni is above the law. In a constitutional democracy, this should not be the case. The President

---

[213] See the Recommendations of the Odoki Commission.

and all government institutions are supposed to be under the law. As an example, Respondents were asked in question 1 section 'A' Question 1 regarding respect to the rule of law in Uganda, respondents rated the respect to rule of law in Uganda as following: 58.14% of the respondents rated rule of law in Uganda as unsatisfactory, 32.56% as Poor and 9.3% as adequate. Those who rated the rule of law in Uganda as unsatisfactory when added together with those who rated rule of law in question 1 as poor, the total is 90.7%. Only 9.3% rated the rule of law in Uganda as adequate and none of the respondents gave the rating of 'Good' or 'Excellent' and that accounts for 0%.

The idea that under the constitution, every actor is subject to the higher law in Uganda is therefore very problematic. Based on the above data, it is clear that that many people in responsible positions are inefficient and cannot deliver because if they cannot respect the constitution or the rule of law, then they are in those positions because of greed as indicated in table 4 of section 'C' of the interviews. Some of the respondents in the interviews argued that many leaders in Uganda are a disgrace in government because many of them are appointed in positions of responsibility being too poor and often overzealous and power drunk. Because of this, they will do anything to bend the rules or even amend the constitution, if necessary, just to stay in power.

It has been found out that absence or weak rule of law and lack of good governance pose a major threat to social and economic development in Uganda, and they have hindered progress in attaining development. Effective and humane justice systems and institutions are fundamental to building societies that facilitate growth and development. Continuing looking at justice in Uganda, in question 7 section 'A' regarding the way Individuals are protected against cruel or excessive punishment, 37.21% rated it as unsatisfactory, 53.49% as poor. Again, if we put together those who rated it as unsatisfactory and those who rated it as poor, the total is 90.7% of all respondents. Only 6.98% of the respondents gave adequate rating. None of the respondents gave 'Good' or 'Excellent' rating and that accounts for 0% of all respondents. 4.65% of the respondents did not answer this question. On question 7 regarding whether respondents agree whether Individuals are free and protected from arbitrary arrest; 76.74% did not agree, 9.3 % agreed. 2.33% of the respondents did not answer this question. On question 9 regarding whether respondents agree that arrested individuals are informed of their rights and brought promptly before a judge to be informed of charges against them; 67.4% did not agree, 18.6% Agreed, and 13.95% did not know.

In regard to the rule of law, the analysis of this study, is supported by a recently published report titled "The World Justice Project Rule of Law Index 2020", in which Uganda was ranked 117 out of 128 countries. The annual report that was released in Washington paints a picture of the rule of law in 128 countries across the globe by providing scores and rankings based on eight factors. The factors include constraints on government powers, absence of corruption, open government, fundamental rights, order and security, regulatory enforcement, civil justice, and criminal justice. The global ranking makes Uganda the worst performing country in the East African region in terms of not adhering to justice and rule of law[214]. The findings in this study does not conflict with the findings of the World Justice Project of Law index 2020.

Table 2 (c): Number in percentage of respondents who rated constitutionalism and the rule of law as unsatisfactory and poor in section 'A'

Question	1	2	3	4	5
Those who rated Unsatisfied and Poor in Percentage	90.7%	81.43%	88.37%	93.02%	93.02%
Question	6	7	8	9	10
Those who rated Unsatisfied and Poor in Percentage	79.07%	90.7%	95.35%	81.39%	95.35%

---

[214] Anthony, Wasaka. *Uganda ranked worst in rule of law, justice.* Daily Monitor Newspaper. Online, 21 April 2021.

Table 2 (d): Number in percentage of respondents who rated constitutionalism and rule of law as adequate in section 'A'

Question	1	2	3	4	5
Adequate	9.3%	13.95%	6.98%	4.65%	4.65%

Question	6	7	8	9	10
Adequate	6.98%	6.98%	2.33%	2.33%	2.33%

Table 2 (e): Number in percentage of respondents who rated constitutionalism as 'Good' or 'Excellent' in section 'A'

Question	1	2	3	4	5
Good or Excellent	0%	2.33%	2.33%	0%	6.98%

Question	6	7	8	9	10
Good or Excellent	0%	0%	2.33%	2.33%	2.33%

Section B: General Data Coding sample

In section B, respondents were asked the following questions below using a scale of 1 to 3 to determine their views on all the ten questions with 1 = Do not Agree; 2 = Agree; 3 = Do not know. However, 0 = Not answered was introduced later to represent questions that were 'not answered or left blank'.

Question 1in section B regarding whether respondents agree or do not agree that the people are the ultimate source of authority of the government and their sovereignty is reflected in the daily realities of the political system in Uganda; 48.84% did not agree, 37.21% agreed and 11.63 % did not know. The question was answered by all respondents. See table 3 (a) below.

On question 2 regarding the 1995 Uganda Constitution, on whether respondents think the executive and legislature behaved in a lawfully justified manner to remove the term limits from the constitution in 2005; 86.05% did not agree, 6.98% agreed, and 6.98% did not know. 2.33% of the respondents, did not answer this question. Only 6.98 of all respondents agreed that the executive and legislature behaved in a lawfully justified manner to remove the term limits from the constitution in 2005; 86.05% did not agree. See table 3 (a) below.

On question 3 regarding whether under the 1995 Uganda Constitution, respondents think the executive and legislature behaved in a lawfully justified manner to remove the age limit cap from the Constitution in 2017; 86.05% did not agree, 6.98% Agreed and 6.98% did not know whether the executive and legislature behaved in a lawfully justified manner to remove the age limit cap from the Constitution in 2017. See table 3 (a) below.

On question 4 regarding whether respondents agree that Key positions in government are contested at regular intervals in Uganda; 53.49% did not agree, 25.58% Agreed, and 20.93% did not know. The question was answered by all respondents. See table 3 (a) below.

On question 5 regarding respondents agree or did not agree that whether the transfer of power is accomplished through orderly and peaceful means in Uganda, 81.4% did not agree, 6.98% agreed and 11.63% did not know. The question was answered by all respondents. See table 3 (a) below.

On question 6 regarding whether respondents agree that Individuals are free to associate with other individuals and groups free from government interference or intimidation; 67.4% did not agree, 20.93% Agreed, and 11.63% did not know. The question was answered by all respondents. See table 3 (a) below.

On question 7 regarding whether respondents agree whether Individuals are free and protected from arbitrary arrest; 76.74% did not agree, 9.3 % agreed. 2.33% of the respondents did not answer this question. See table 3 (a) below.

On question 8 regarding whether respondents agree that generally there is equality before the law in Uganda; 76.74% did not agree, and 13.95% agreed. 9.3% did not know. The question was answered by all respondents. See table 3 (a) below.

On question 9 regarding whether respondents agree that arrested individuals are informed of their rights and brought promptly before a judge to be informed of charges against them; 67.4% did not agree, 18.6% Agreed, and 13.95% did not know. The question was answered by all respondents. See table 3 (a) below.

On question 10 regarding whether respondents agree that everyone in Uganda has a right to freedom of opinion and expression and the right to seek, receive, and impart information and ideas through any media; 67.4% did not agree, 23.3% agreed, and 9.3% did not know. The question was answered by all respondents. See table 3 (a)below.

Table 3 (a) below, shows how people responded to the questions in section 'B':

Table 3 (a): Section 'B' General sample data coding.

Respondents	Questions										Respondents	Questions									
	1	2	3	4	5	6	7	8	9	10		1	2	3	4	5	6	7	8	9	10
1	1	1	1	3	1	2	2	2	1	2	23	1	1	1	3	1	1	1	1	1	2
2	2	1	1	2	1	1	1	1	1	2	24	1	1	1	3	1	1	1	1	1	1
3	2	1	1	1	1	1	1	1	1	2	25	2	2	2	2	2	2	2	2	2	2
4	1	1	1	1	1	1	1	1	1	1	26	2	1	1	1	1	1	1	1	1	2
5	1	1	1	1	1	1	1	1	1	1	27	1	1	1	2	1	1	1	1	2	1
6	1	1	1	1	1	1	1	1	1	1	28	2	1	1	2	1	1	1	1	1	1
7	3	1	1	1	3	3	1	1	2	1	29	2	1	1	2	2	2	1	1	1	2
8	2	1	1	1	1	1	1	1	1	1	30	1	1	1	1	1	1	1	1	1	1
9	2	1	1	1	1	1	1	1	2	2	31	0	2	3	3	3	3	3	3	3	1
10	1	1	1	2	1	1	1	1	1	1	32	3	1	1	1	1	1	3	3	3	3
11	2	1	1	2	1	1	1	1	1	1	33	1	1	1	1	1	1	1	1	1	1
12	2	1	2	2	1	2	1	1	3	1	34	2	1	1	1	1	1	2	2	1	1
13	1	1	1	1	1	1	1	1	1	1	35	2	1	1	1	1	3	1	2	2	1
14	1	1	1	1	1	1	1	1	1	1	36	2	1	1	1	1	3	3	2	2	1
15	1	1	1	2	1	2	1	1	1	1	37	3	1	3	2	2	1	1	1	1	1
16	1	1	1	1	1	2	1	1	1	1	38	2	1	1	1	3	3	3	1	2	1
17	1	1	1	2	1	1	1	1	1	1	39	1	1	1	1	1	1	1	0	1	1
18	3	1	1	3	1	2	2	1	3	1	40	2	1	1	3	3	3	3	2	2	1
19	1	1	1	3	1	1	1	1	1	1	41	1	1	1	1	1	2	1	1	1	1
20	1	3	3	1	1	1	1	1	3	3	42	1	1	1	1	1	2	1	1	1	1
21	3	1	1	3	3	1	1	3	3	3	43	2	2	2	2	1	1	1	1	1	2
22	1	1	1	3	1	1	1	3	1	2											

In Section B, all the 10 questions have something to do with Constitutionalism and the rule of law. According to the data received, the table 3 (b) below shows the percentages of respondents who did not agree with the statement that matters raised were handled in a manner of constitutionalism and according to the rule of law.

Table 3 (b): Number of respondents who did not agree with the statements in questions 1 to 10 in section 'B' of the questionnaire

Question	1	2	3	4	5
Not Agree in percentage	48.84%	86.05%	86.05%	53.49%	81.4%
Question	6	7	8	9	10
Not Agree in percentage	67.4%	76.74%	76.74%	67.4%	67.4%

Table 3 (c): Number of respondents who agreed with the statements in questions 1 – 10 in section 'B' of the questionnaire

Question	1	2	3	4	5
Those who Agreed in Percentage	37.21%	6.98%	6.98%	25.58%	6.98%
Question	6	7	8	9	10
Those who Agreed in Percentage	20.93%	9.3%	13.95%	18.6%	23.3%

Table 3 (d): Number of respondents who felt that they did not know in questions 1-10 section 'B' of the questionnaire

Question	1	2	3	4	5
Those who did not know in percentage	11.63%	6.98%	6.98%	20.98%	11.63%
Question	6	7	8	9	10
Those who did not know in percentage	11.63%	2.33%	9.3%	13.95%	9.3%

Table 3 (e) Summarises all information in section B in percentages.

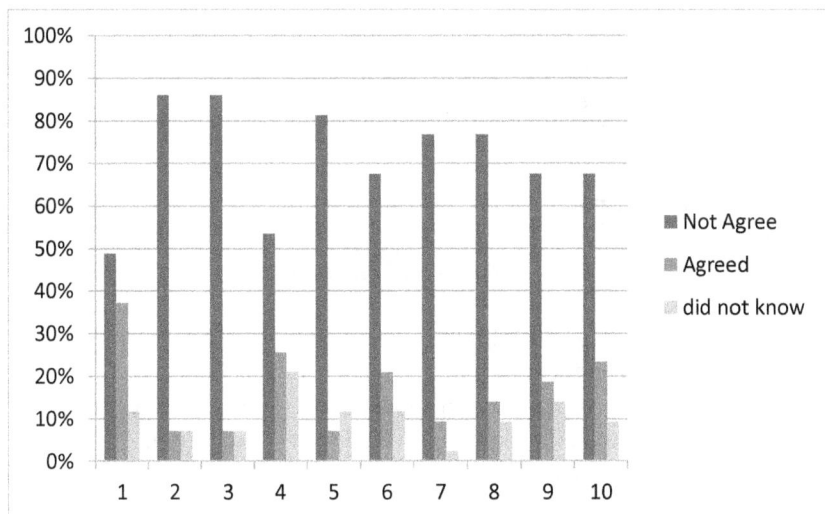

Section C: Interview deliberations

Section 'C' Deliberations

Question 1 deliberations':

- Since Independence, Uganda never had democracy and there is no democracy at all in Uganda today.
- Democracy died in 1966 when Obote suspended the Uganda Constitution. Since then, there is no democracy in Uganda.
- Freedom of speech taken away in Uganda and people are scared.
- Government is filled with corruption.
- The Police still undermine the Constitution and rule of law. For example, the Constitutional court ruled that the public management Act was unconstitutional, but the Police is still enforcing it as against the court's ruling.
- Arbitrary arrests for the opposition are a clear indication that there no democracy in Uganda.
- Democracy in Uganda is a showcase, where leaders pretend that they have been democratically elected.
- No democracy now, Uganda has never attained democracy.
- Democracy has failed in Uganda.
- Democracy in Uganda is just on paper, the principles of democracy are not observed.

- Democracy applies only to those who are pro-government.

Question 2 deliberations':

- No rule of law in Uganda.
- No Judicial and Police integrity
- Leaders only do things only according to how they aim to benefit.
- The laws made, do not benefit the people but those in power.
- The laws are there but violated by those who are supposed to implement them.
- People operate on orders of the president and not according to the law.
- Museveni is the law.
- Other institutions like the Judiciary cannot do well their work because of intimidation from the executive.
- There is no clear separation of powers between the three arms of government. The other two are controlled by the executive.
- NRM government above the law.
- The rule of law in Uganda today is active but in favour of the ruling Party.
- The laws are there, but not given due respect by some individuals including leaders.
- The rule of law is not respected in Uganda but it's on case-to-case basis.

Question 3 deliberations':

- Justice only belongs to the privileged and wealthy.
- Justice in Uganda long disappeared and ceased to carry any meaning.
- Justice is not being observed.
- Justice in Uganda had started seeing some light but now that light is completely out.
- If you have no money for bribe, it is impossible to win a court case under the current government.
- For the majority, instead of justice, there is injustice.
- There is arrest of individuals on unknown grounds and unfair hearings in court.
- Judges are not independent since they are appointed by the president.
- There have been some good judges who have made significant rulings even the system is corrupted. But the good judges have been hunted and intimidated by the military.
- Justice in Uganda is served depending on who you know in the corridors of power.
- It is strongly recommended that the president should not appoint the chief justice because that makes them complacent. New mechanisms need to be introduced on how to appoint judges.

Question 4 deliberations':

- No human rights in Uganda.
- People cannot exercise their democratic right to elect leaders of their choice. Elections are organised and then rigged.
- Rise in unlawful and arbitrary killings.
- Rights of Ugandans are stepped upon.
- Many people are not aware that many of their rights are being violated. Human rights sensitisation for the population is highly recommended.
- Violence, intimidation and restriction on rights and freedoms.
- The underprivileged and the poor are not protected by the law.
- People's rights are everyday violated as they are arrested and put in ungazetted prisons for torture.
- Civilians are being tried in military courts as is with the current case of NUP supporters.
- There are no human rights in Uganda especially if you belong to the opposition.
- The NRM government has gained prominence in abductions, torture, and killings of innocent citizens for political reasons.
- Human rights do not work in Uganda.
- There is continued human rights violation in Uganda that include very poor health services, lack of education facilities and the closing of spaces of expression like the internet (social media etc).

Question 5 (a) deliberations':

- The lifting of term limits was an insult to Ugandans.
- It was done to benefit the sitting president.
- No respect to constitutionalism and rule of law in Uganda.
- Promoting dictatorship.
- inspired by greed for power.
- People were taken as idiots and thoughts of Ugandans were ignored.
- It would have been okay if the term limits were lifted in the interest of the people and not the incumbent.
- Having a good constitution is not a guarantee for good governance. It involves much more than having just a good constitution.

Question 5 (b) deliberations':

- The removal of the age limit cap paved way for life presidency.
- It was done against the will of the majority.
- It needed a referendum.
- SFC highjacked parliament and beat up members of parliament.
- MPs did not remove the age limit cap willingly, they were beaten and then bribed with 29 million each.

- Those in power think that they are the only ones entitled to rule.
- Some think it was okay because it opened as well for the young people to contest.
- The removal of the cap on the age limit was the worst idea by the NRM government on democracy and rule of law.

Question 5 (c) deliberations':

- The 1995 Constitution is not there to serve the people.
- The Constitution is there to serve the leaders.
- Serving the government, instead of the people.
- The 1995 constitution of Uganda is meant to serve the citizens of Uganda, but ironically, it is serving only the ruling Party and government officials.
- The current constitution serves the head of state and his cabinet.

Question 6 deliberations':

- The 1995constitution serves the NRM government and President Museveni, no consideration for the people.
- The Constitution gives absolute powers to the president which the president uses to amend any article in the constitution which may not favour their long stay.
- The Ugandan Constitution is very vulnerable and does not provide the endurance needed in a constitution.
- Serves only the western part of Uganda.
- Just on paper and only used when serving the interests of specific people in government.
- Incumbent leaders even when they lose elections, they find a way to rig elections to keep themselves in power.
- There is no doubt that the Ugandan constitution is abused by a few individuals but otherwise does most of its functions as the Constitution of Uganda.

In conclusion of this chapter, based on those findings, the Constitution in Uganda is therefore being perceived more and more as meaningless and disregarded by those in authority. The idea that a constitution is a people's document, has become to be very contentious as a constitution is no longer perceived as a 'people's document' but rather as an elite-driven process that does not respect the ideas of the people.

Findings, Recommendations and Conclusion

Findings

'The constitution' as a document and the 'rule of law', with other laws apart from the constitution included, based on the findings, people are generally of a view that the constitution and other laws are not taken into consideration for example when people are being appointed in positions of leadership and when it is done, it is rather ceremonial than based on the constitution as the law of the land. in question 1 section 'A' Question 1 regarding respect to the rule of law in Uganda, respondents rated the respect to rule of law in Uganda as following: 58.14% of the respondents rated rule of law in Uganda as unsatisfactory, 32.56% as Poor and 9.3% as adequate. One of the arguments provided is that in Uganda, it is not being in line with the law that matters, but rather belonging to a certain ethnic or political group is what matters. If the law is not resected, its existence provides very little meaning.

As a finding, the Constitution in Uganda is limited and one such limitation of applicability is around ethnicity. The culture of constitutional making has so far failed to address the challenges associated with tribal and ethnicity alignment. Liberal democracy based on individualism has tended to result into tribal or ethnic alliance of survival rather than in national interest to develop democratic values of tolerance to diverse views, a spirit of compromise, acceptance of majority views while respecting the minority. In question 2 for example regarding the protection of law in Uganda, considering whether it is free from discrimination on race, ethnicity, gender, class, socio-economic status etc. 39.53% rated it as unsatisfactory, 41.9% as poor, 13.95% as Adequate, 2.33% rated it as 'Good'.

Since the existence of written constitutions have failed to result into strong institutions as in terms of applicability, as a result the 'strong man/woman syndrome' has taken root in Uganda and has dominated the democratic institutions provided for in the Constitution resulting into very weak or non-functioning institutions. This further has provided room for a culture of violence to be instituted in the Ugandan system. Successive governments in Uganda have survived on the control of the means of violence; thus, any agitation is often met with official violence. In question 7 section 'A' for example regarding the way Individuals are protected against cruel or excessive punishment, 37.21% rated it as unsatisfactory, 53.49% as poor. Uganda has a constitution, but the constitution is not performing it duty properly. This has resulted into unconstitutional struggles for political power and control of state resources and according to the findings, it is the cause of instability in terms of peace and social order in Uganda.

As a result of the study, it has been found that countries with very weak institutions like Uganda are most likely to disregard constitutionalism and rule of law. If Uganda is compared to Norwayor German as an example, one would find that election violence and human rights abuses are more likely to occur in Uganda than in Norway or Germany. Further, if comparison is made between Uganda, the DRC, or Ivory Coast, all of which are countries with very weak institutions, then one would find that there is not much difference in likelihood for election violence or human rights abuses that may occur.

As a negative implication, the finding is that the failure of constitutionalism and the rule of law, has resulted into corruption in the Ugandan system. Since many government officials have been cited in corruption deals and not punished as according to the laws of Uganda, but instead promoted, has resulted into the erosion of public trust in the public sector. In the interviews, respondents pointed out issues like; there is no law in Uganda, the laws made do not benefit the people, but instead those in power, the laws are there, but violated by those who are supposed to implement them etc. see table 3 of section C above for respondents' comments.

Further to the above as a finding, there is excessive indiscipline in government departments in Uganda, and lack of action by the government and its agencies on reported cases of acts of indiscipline has encouraged corruption among government officials, political fanaticism, lack of concern for the people's welfare, conflicting rules, and regulations, poor management of resources and lack of good governance. Noncompliance of members with rules and regulations, resulting in disorderly behaviour and impunity is order of the day contrary to what is expected in a constitutional democracy and under the rule of law. In addition, also as a finding, poor management on the part of those at the helm of government and public affairs is another cause of indiscipline, abuse of rights of others and none respect to the laws of Uganda. In question 3 for example regarding limits on the powers of government which elected officials must obey; 34.88% rated it as unsatisfactory, 53.49% as poor, 6.98% rated it as adequate, 2.33% gave a good rating.

As a result, many opportunists have found themselves in the corridors of power on the basis that their party is at the centre. In Uganda, mostly it is all about the Party and not democracy, the rule of law or constitutionalism. Constitutionalism that could have served as a constraint in these kinds of cases, is absent and there is therefore bound to be maladministration of things in the state. As a negative implication, it results in not paving way for the smooth running of the state affairs and act of discipline. Acts of impunity result into lawlessness, which is not motivational factor for the citizen in Uganda and instead discourages people. See the feedback in in all the sections.

Apart from people being picked up and locked in safe and tortured because of their political beliefs and alignment, people detained without being produced before the courts etc., there is also further human rights abuses like those with power or authority stealing of citizens land and other properties thus turning citizens into refugees in their own country due to impunity which is rampant in Uganda and clearly against the rule of law. The impoverished peasants cannot win court cases either they cannot afford it, or the courts are already compromised because of corruption (see results in question 2 above regarding equal protection of law and question 6 section 'A' regarding the administration of justice in Uganda).

With all available evidence, the authorities in Uganda still insist that Uganda is a constitutional democracy. Even within Uganda itself, democracy and the rule of law remain as relative ideas. Any constitution to have meaning, it must perform its function. The conclusion that can be reached in regard with the constitution, is that "not every state that has a constitution is a constitutional democracy." The state may have a written constitution like in the case of Uganda and be a constitutional autocracy rather than a constitutional democracy.

Another important finding of the study is that democracy does not necessarily guarantee the rule of law. It is a misconception to state that a constitutional democracy can generally result into the rule of law. Many people think that 'democracy' is synonymous with the 'rule of law'. Having carefully looked at the results of the case study, I find it difficult to agree with this kind of generalisation. Instead, I propose that democracy and rule of law can relative ideas even if law is understood terms of 'what is'. When it comes to the rule of law, it is common knowledge that many African leaders have ruled their people with an iron fist with very little regard to the constitution, the rule of law, democracy, and human rights. Based on the findings, the majority of respondents do not agree or rated questions regarding to human rights as unsatisfactory or poor. As a finding, there has been an onslaught on the rule of law in Uganda and atrocities have allegedly been committed by government and those holding positions of authority.

The need to make a distinction between 'democracy' and 'rule of law' is based on the idea that democracy does not necessarily result into the 'rule of law'. In the same way, the 'rule of law' does not necessarily result into a 'democratic system'. Constitutions contain the fundamental and most often referred to as the supreme law of the state, and the rule of law dictates the enforcement of those principles above all other laws. Question 1 in section B regarding whether respondents agree or do not agree as an example that the people are the ultimate source of authority of any democratic government and their sovereignty is reflected in the daily realities of the political system in Uganda; 48.84% did not agree, 37.21% agreed and 11.63 % did not know.

Constitutions also preserve fundamental principles and values by making the process of amendment burdensome. However, this boils down to the function ability of the supreme law. As a negative implication, thin forms of constitutionalism can enable undemocratic authority to claim legitimacy from the constitution while people's views for example on the drafting of the 1995 Uganda Constitution, people's views were easily ignored and the random amendment of it to suit the likes of those in authority. Further again as a negative implication, if that happens, it means that the Constitution in a practical sense is not a people's document. In question 2 section B regarding the 1995 Uganda Constitution for example, on whether respondents think the executive and legislature behaved in a lawfully justified manner to remove the term limits from the constitution in 2005; 86.05% did not agree, 6.98% agreed, and 6.98% did not know.

In the case of Uganda and probably other African states, there is lack of a clear understanding of the principle of law. Many Africans still interpret the law as a command of the sovereign and that is why the president and other top government officials are perceived as above or the law unto themselves. It has therefore become a norm that governments in Uganda are based on the person of the president rather than the principle of law. This is the basis on which the idea is formulated that President Museveni is the fountain of honour and anyone in need of anything in Uganda, must obey him.

As part of the problem, this paper looked at one of the arguments or ideas in current studies, that 'not every state that has a constitution (in that sense) is a constitutional state'. Based on the findings, it can be rightly argued that the Ugandan Constitution, is not there to serve the people of Uganda, but rather a tool used to by leaders to legitimise their stay in power. Based on the findings and as a negative implication, although the Ugandan Constitution is referred to as a people's document, but in practical terms, it is not. When respondents were asked questions relating to the constitution for example, most of them did not agree that the Ugandan constitution is indeed a people's document. The ongoing argument put forward by some constitutional analysts that some are facade/sham constitutions, in that they exist for 'cosmetic' purposes only and have no effect in reality, the argument is proved to be valid based on the findings.

Based on the findings of the study, the 'unofficial emerging theory' that the legislature and judiciary are increasingly becoming rubber stamps for the executive in majoritarian democracies in Africa and playing a key role in the executive's prolonged hold on power can now be confirmed. It is rightly argued that instead of being independent in the exercise their constitutional powers, the legislature and Judiciary have turned into string puppets dancing on the tune of the executive. Uganda can be identified with a fascist regime parliament and the judiciary where they are only manipulated tools for dictators to carry out their despotic will. Since ethnicity and political belonging is of greater importance in Uganda, those appointed in positions of leadership see no reason why they should live by that constitution. If we take question 4 regarding the idea that each arm or branch of government has adequate power to check the powers of other branches, 41.86% rated it as unsatisfactory, 51.16% rated it as poor.

During the interviews, examples were cited by respondents as in the case of judges who are always compromised by the executive and fail to offer justice. One of the main problems cited is that high court judges in Uganda are presidential appointees and therefore makes it difficult to freely offer justice without being compromised; neither can they hold the executive in check as according to the ideas of separation of powers and that of checks and balances. The population therefore rightly thinks that hight court judges pay allegiance to the appointing authority rather than the people or the constitution.

In Constitutional democracies, the judiciary which applies the law to individual cases, acts as the guardian of the rule of law. Thus, an independent and properly functioning judiciary is a perquisite for the rule of law which require a just legal system, the right to fair hearing and access to justice of which, it is not the case in Uganda. In question 6 section A for example regarding the administration of Justice in Uganda, 25.58% rated it as unsatisfactory, 53.49% as poor.

The Ugandan constitution as the supreme law, is therefore seen in the light of being manipulated to support elite political leaders.

Based on the findings, the Ugandan constitution does not function as it ought to have and this has resulted into many associated problems for Ugandans e.g., political, economic, social etc. It is understandable that constitutions under a constitutional democracy, are made by 'men, not gods therefore mistakes or omissions are likely to occur. In question 3 section B regarding whether under the 1995 Uganda Constitution, respondents think the executive and legislature behaved in a lawfully justified manner to remove the age limit cap from the Constitution in 2017; 86.05% did not agree, 6.98% Agreed and 6.98% did not know whether the executive and legislature behaved in a lawfully justified manner to remove the age limit cap from the Constitution in 2017.

In addition, societal needs change with time and may require constitutional amendments. Therefore, constitutional amendment is a normal process which aims to correct imperfections in the existing instrument. However, it should never be used lightly to benefit incumbent leaders. The process of amendment was designed to be burdensome so as to make sure that it is done properly and in the interest of the people. The findings of this study support the existing idea that constitutions need to be sufficiently flexible to allow future generations to respond to various political, economic, social, and other changes. It is also important however, that constitutions must be sufficiently burdensome to amend in the sense that they must be stable and show signs of consistency in order to allow participants to anticipate their acts' consequences.

The test should be that a constitution should never be amended solely in the interest/s of the sitting leader for example aimed at the extension of their stay in office beyond the constitutional prescribed duration. Such amendments can be distinguished from aments aimed at the benefit of the people directly. Law cannot be law if it is not stable and predictable. If the law keeps on being amended or changed to suit an individual or group of principled men, then the law is no longer serving its original function but rather now kidnapped and used as a tool by those holding political power. The law cannot function well if it is not consistent; the function ability is found in its consistence.

Depending on what one understands by the 'rule of law', but, it can be rightly argued that the 'rule of law' can exist in any other systems of government other than a democracy as already mentioned above as in the case of 'Communist China'. It wouldnt make very good sense to argue that because China is not a democracy based on western values, understanding and intepretation and therefore, there is no rule of law in China. It is indeed true that the rule of law is a fundamental principle embraced in most modern democracies. however, it does not mean that every labelled constitutional democracy embraces the rule of law in reality.

The above, re-affirms my proposal and argument of the relativity of the idea of democracy and rule of law. The Chinese can argue for example that the Chinese state is a 'socialist democracy' in which the Chinese Communist Party is the central authority that acts in the interest of the people and approves which political parties can run. If democracy means participation of different political parties in elections within a specified period by the constitution, then Uganda can be classified as a democratic state. However, the argument remains that elections alone, cannot guarantee democracy neither the rule of law.

Democracy means much more than the participation of the people in elections and politics. In question 5 section 'B' regarding respondents agree or did not agree that whether the transfer of power is accomplished through orderly and peaceful means in Uganda, 81.4% did not agree, 6.98% agreed and 11.63% did not know. Democracy needs to go further to the protection of human rights of all citizens applying the laws that are already in place and where there is a need, making new other laws to include new situations that were not anticipated before. But the laws should not be intended at the curbing of rights of citizens.

In most constitutional democracies, the standard is the 'constitution' but when the constitution fails in its function ability, the standard is no longer there as a guarantee. As an example, those who rated the rule of law in Uganda as unsatisfactory when added together with those who rated rule of law in question 1 section A as poor, the total is 90.7%. Only 9.3% rated the rule of law in Uganda as adequate and none of the respondents gave the rating of 'Good' or

'Excellent'. The constitution as a supreme law can fail but it does not mean that all the other laws cannot function. This makes me conclude that it is important to make a distinction between democracy and the rule of law and not to confuse one as the other. The understanding of democracy and the rule of law can be relative.

The implication is that democracy and rule of law are both distinct and relative terms and in order to understand them clearly, much more need to be taken into consideration than a generalised value approach. If one person is living in China which is a communist state but has for example the basics of life like food, reasonable shelter, medicine, work, family life etc. that individual may be living a much more fulfilled life than a person living in the UK for example, but with no right to family life, work, healthcare, housing etc. But if someone is living in Uganda where the individual cannot find work, food, or get good healthcare, most likely to be picked up at any time, imprisoned and tortured etc. What does 'democracy' and 'rule of law' mean to the three individuals? In all the three cases, democracy and rule of law can be relative.

Based on the findings, the idea that a constitutional democracy is a system that can guarantee the rule of law is distorted, fraud and so much generalised. In question 9 regarding the way people feel individual rights to life, liberty, and protection of property are guaranteed by the due process of the law, 51.16% rated it as unsatisfactory, 30.23% as poor. Adding those who rated it as unsatisfactory to those who rated it as poor, the total is 81.39%. Only 2.33% gave adequate rating and the same 2.33% gave 'Good' rating. None gave 'Excellent' rating. Democracy as system has got many flaws and has been corrupted in so many ways to suit the needs of those who hold power.

Democracy, the constitution, and rule of law should all be understood as living ideas which means that they are capable of changing or evolving. They are not constant, stagnant, nor universal. Under any constitutional democracy, the idea of rule of law and respect to human rights may be perceived differently in different countries and cultures. The NRM government for example presents itself as a democratic government, following the rule of law. However, when people were asked about their opinions regarding democracy and rule of law most of them were of a view that there is no democracy or rule of law in Uganda. The different interpretation and understanding reinforces my opinion that what is referred to as a constitutional democracy, rule of law, constitutionalism etc are all relative ideas which means that they are not absolute.

As a finding, in Uganda, there is a disregard to societal values and norms as a consequence of having a constitution without constitutionalism and it is a negative implication. Different communities in Uganda used to have values and norms that were disregarded in favour of constitutionalism. However, constitutionalism based on western values approach, has been taken out of context and so far, failed as in the sense of practice.

In the recently concluded elections that took place on 14 January 2021 as an example, there has been widespread allegations of kidnappings, torture of political opponents, and killings of opposition figures. Civilians have been detained as political prisoners in military barracks, disappearance of citizens especially from the opposition side, criminalisation of the practice of journalism, serial killings of women, land grabbing etc. question 7 regarding whether respondents agree whether Individuals are free and protected from arbitrary arrest; 76.74% did not agree, 9.3 % agreed. These findings are supported by data whether it has to do with constitutionalism, rule of law or respect and protection of human rights.

Recommendations

As a recommendation, people in Uganda, must stop seeing as demi-gods who should be worshiped by citizens. This gives leaders a wrong perception of themselves and the office they hold. It is like in the words of one of Africa's great writers Chinua Achebe who said that "African leaders see themselves as the ones holding the sword and at the same time, the yam. The slice one gets from a leader, depends on how well one behaves before that leader." It is imperative that the powers of the president in Uganda, need to be trimmed and a mechanism put in place whereby a balance of power is created and having practical means in place of the possibility of sacking the president if found guilty of gross misconduct. That would encourage accountability and reduce on paternalistic and nepotistic behaviour. This need to be extended to all other public office holders. Legislation as a matter of 'must' be strengthened in areas where public office is likely to be abused and mechanisms put in place that the legislation is not rendered impotent by those holding offices.

The very first thing Ugandans must do is to make sure that the constitution and other laws established perform their duties in practice. The law must be held as the sovereign, the supreme and highest power in the land and should never be over-ruled by a president or the sitting government. The law must prevail as long as it complies with the requirements of justice. In short, the constitution must be authoritative, and its sovereignty must be accepted as correct and proper and as unchallenged.

Democracy cannot guarantee the rule of law as evidenced in the case of Uganda, but the laws well established can guarantee democracy and its values. The biggest problem for Uganda is the office of the president. There is therefore an urgent need for Ugandans to deconstruct power based on strongman/woman leadership. I recommend that the office of the president should be ceremonial, limited to one term and made rotational based on ethnic groups in Uganda. In the place of strong wo/man leader, Ugandans should aim to build strong institutions aimed to serve all citizen equally and also encourage a professional civil service, even if the presidency is constitutionally rotated every five years.

Given as the case of Uganda, if a professional civil service for example is firmly put in place and not dependent on the person or office of the president, but rather on the constitution, then the change of the person at the top, does not affect anything as long as the law is upheld and obeyed. This has the implication that unless until the time when the citizens in countries like Uganda are able to influence the direction of national affairs and not dictated by those in power, we may then not have a functioning constitutional democracy.

In a modern society, it is wrong for power to be concentrated only in the hands of the President. True leadership and not puppet leadership can be provided at different levels of society meaning that people have a say in decision making and policy development. It starts from the bottom and then upwards but cannot be from up to the bottom. This defies the laws of nature even a tree grows from bottom upwards and needs sustenance by the roots. I recommend that it is time to use African innovation in politics and in terms of leadership mechanisms as welll on how to address corruption and abuse of power.

Any society to thrive, that society must have strong institutions. Increasingly weak institutions can only perform their duties at the consent of the one holding centralised power. In Uganda and other African states, constitutions were abrogated because the institutions that were in place were too weak and could not hold to account those who abrogated the constitution. Laws can only work where there are strong institutions to enforce them. Constitutional democratic governments must be subject to a number of checks and balances. It is not possible to have a constitutional democracy without functional checks and balances. At the moment, Uganda's checks and balances are just a label in name and bearing very little meaning. Power must therefore be embedded in institutions and not individuals.

As a means of proper separation of powers, I recommend that instead of the legislature having the final say on the constitutionality of their own legislation as in most majoritarian democracies, laws in Uganda should be subject to a judicial review of their constitutionality by the supreme or constitutional court in order to build consensus. Since judges are supposed to be independent, they should not be presidential appointees. Uganda has to think of a constitutional procedure whereby judges are appointed to office, but not by the seating president. As a way of addressing the problem, the legal and parliamentary committee for example, can select names of potential judges and then parliament can confirm or reject them. Uganda does not need a unitary and centralised government, and as a recommendation, I suggest that Uganda follows the path of federal and decentralised system government where power is shared among stake holders.

It is therefore very important to be able to make a distinction between democracy as a system and the rule of law. At the moment, democracy and ruled of law are used in a synonymous way. I would like to argue that democracy as a system and the rule of law are two different things. If these two were exactly the same, where one would have constitutional democracy, it would automatically result into the rule of law. based on the findings of this study, this is not the case. The mistake often made, is to think that having a constitutional democracy, automatically will lead to the rule of law. I differ from the position generally held by most people that constitutional democracy means rule of law. The reason for me why I differ is that there are numerous examples of countries thought to be constitutional democracies and yet do not uphold the rule of law.

It is therefore recommended that Ugandans and other fragile democracies ought to understand that the rule of law can exist in any other system other than a constitutional democracy. My problem here is to make constitutional democracy "the rule of law". Depending on the society in question, one can find out that the rule of law can function much better in a constitutional monarchy much better probably than in a constitutional democracy. While democracy is a competition of ideas, the law should be general not discriminate, prospective open and clear and working for the good and benefit of everyone in that society.

As a recommendation, Uganda needs to have a well-founded constitutional order that must set out clearly how the state must be organised and not have a sham constitution intended for donor nations and not for the people of Uganda. How the state is organised and how it functions is a matter of law and not democracy. Democracy is just a system of government of choosing and replacing the government through free and fair elections and participation of the people. But this has to be in accordance with the laws already established and such laws should be open, stable, clear and the general rules should govern executive laws- making. As a recommendation, instead of insisting on democracy in Uganda which has blatantly failed, the focus should instead be on building a system based on laws that works as a way of collective decisions and steering societies in a particular direction like China has managed to achieve.

The understanding must be clear on the general rule that any constitution, must have two sides in the same way a legal tender coin. It is the two sides forming one that makes it legal tender. The recommendation therefore is the constitution must have two important but inseparable sides. On one side, a constitution has to be flexible meaning that it is flexible enough to allow future changes possible. On the second side, the constitution must be inflexible enough so as not to allow spontaneous changes that can result into the erosion of constitutional authority and stability.

On this basis as in the case of Uganda, I recommend a more rigid and fixed side of the constitution to be applied in Uganda, but not so much with the intention that the rigidity forms the breeding ground for it to be overthrown. Therefore, it should be only in special circumstances that the flexible side of the constitution is presented for any changes to be made, but the exercise should not be lightly carried out and therefore, if necessary, it has to be done with the help of judicial interpretation or a referendum depending on the importance of the matter.

The constitution should only be changed by extraordinary majority based on consensus rather than a simple majority in parliament. The constitution as a foundational law, is different from other laws that can be passed with a simple majority. But this also has problems because many of the dominant parties in majoritarian democracies like Uganda, dominate parliament which makes it easy for them to change the constitution. I therefore recommend that it is necessary for Ugandans to find a balance between the flexibility and inflexibility of the constitution bearing in mind that constitutions are not immutable documents frozen in time, but rather a living document that is capable of growing and developing.

The balance is so important because it helps the constitution establish a stable framework that works so that it is not easily amendable for it to lose meaning as seen with the 1995 Uganda constitution. By failing to strike that balance, the Ugandan constitution has become a play toy for the shrewd and self-deserving executive. It is not by coincidence that Uganda's history is indeed replete with constitutional crises, civil wars, military coups, insurgencies, ethnic/religious/political cleavages, and violent unconstitutional regime changes all of which have caused constitutional instability and no respect to the rule of law.

As a recommendation, it must be understood that democracy, constitutionalism, and the rule of law extends beyond formal institutions of government and includes incudes societal values and customs as well. Ugandans and Africans need to understand that good governance is not about a system or a structure but can also be achieved in so many other different ways and is it is mainly about the attitudes and good political intentions which can result into political stability. If the people's attitudes and political intentions are good, it is the base on which democracy and constitutionalism can be built and not the other way round. Africans thought that by copying and establishing a democratic structure will automatically result into democratic values like the rule of law, respect to human rights etc. But the introduction of democracy in many African countries and discarding African values and customs has resulted into extreme violence and human rights abuses.

One of the challenges that has been often put forward by sceptics of Uganda and Africa's ability to manage democratically, is the challenge of managing ethnic relations. Sceptics are saying that Uganda and other African countries are failing because of ethnic clashes. However, as an implication, democracy has a hand in fuelling ethnic tensions as it emphasizes that the majority have their way but prescribing no practical solutions to the minority at times when put together can actually form the majority. In my opinion, 'ethnic relations' is not as complicated as we are often made to believe. It takes commitment, focus, and a democratic disposition to respond appropriately.

Some measures that have been used to manage ethnic relations including racial relations I can recommend include good governance is a product of good social relations; federalism, or special political arrangements to protect minorities and vulnerable groups, including autonomy arrangements; affirmative action to allow weaker or smaller groups an opportunity to be part of the system; zoning, or power rotation arrangements to give hope and meaning to the place and role of all ethnic groups; multiculturalism, a deliberate programme designed to ensure autonomy of cultures and cultural interaction as state policy; political appointments and balancing to ensure equal opportunity; political and administrative decentralization, mostly away from the major urban centres. This reduces pressures on the centre, disperses responsibility, and builds a sense of belonging; legal provisions against discrimination, hate crimes and statements, and all forms of cultural discrimination etc.

In the pre-independence and democratic Uganda, people of different tribes for example moved into Buganda to find work and were peacefully settled, were given land, and allowed to marry within the Baganda. In Buganda then, there was a system based on Ubuntu (Obuntu bulamu) philosophy and values and ethnicity then was not a problem. There are societal values that used to exist in Uganda that no longer exist or exist but have been greatly diluted due to the introduction of the idea of constitution and rule of law and ignoring or negating social values and norms.

Constitutionalism that disregards societal values and norms operates in a vacuum and fails to incorporate the strings that bind the people together. African people for example are communitarian, and their philosophy is based on communitarianism. Western philosophy on the other hand is mainly about the individualism and individual rights. The challenge Africa is facing, is the failure to merge the two extremes together. Competition and most often unfair competition introduced by democracy without taking into consideration African values has resulted into a boiling pot of anger and violence because some people see no other way of achieving justice. Constitutional democracy should have been gradual and transformative of the already existing values in Uganda and other African nations rather than as dismantling. There is also a need to re-introduce societal values and norms in Uganda and as well as in other African communities that do not contradict with values of of modern era constitutionalism and democracy but can help discipline and re-direct the behaviour of the present and future generations.

With the introduction of constitutional democracy, African way of life and values, were labelled bad and backward and therefore discarded. Most importantly and as a recommendation, response policies must be anticipatory and not always responsive, after the facts have happened. Further, there is a need to find ways of reviving some of African values and customs alongside modern democracy and constitutionalism. It is therefore recommended that democracy must be understood that it cannot exist in a vacuum, but rather it has to be established and built on the existing societal values and then the democratic values enhance societal values and not the other way round. We all know that the interactions and engagements between the various ethnic groups can only be to the benefit of all if truly well managed. In the past for example Ubuntu philosophy made Africans reach out even to strangers.

Sceptics may argue that the re-introduction of African way of life based on African values and customs cannot work because it is voluntary and not law. Although adherence to this kind of rule is voluntary, but society had a way of sanctioning erring individuals who indulged for example in any of the following: gross unfaithfulness, dishonesty, laziness, lack of commitment to organisation and nation, anxiety to attain great height without works worth, lack of trust etc. The respect of societal values and norms enabled people to live peacefully and help one another since all knew such values. it is like queuing in shops and supermarkets in the UK, it is not a law but a societal value everyone know and respects. Since societal values were and are embedded in everyday lives of the people, everyone knows that in order to be part of a particular community or society, one had to abide by them.

Citing Mazrui once again, he argued that although Africa can never completely go back to its pre-colonial starting point, it is recommended that there may be a case for re-establishing contacts with familiar landmarks of modernisation under indigenous impetus. As an insight, constitutional democracy did not overthrow the entire British culture; it was rather used to transform that needed to be transformed, but within the existing British culture. In the same way, constitutionalism can be used to transform and not to overthrow African culture, custom and values. I recommend that future African studies conduct further investigation in form of study on this. African leaders must search their hearts, look at the faces of the elders, women and children and decide what is best.

As a recommendation, Constitution development and the making of laws must be an ongoing exercise in that people continue to dialogue and consult amongst the diverse groups and communities on what societal values as a particular group they are willing to compromise on and which ones need to be promoted under constitutionalism and rule of law in order to build more consensus.

The idea is to focus on values that can be held in common rather than those that divide the people. Africans must stop seeing government as means of control, but rather of possession of capacity to achieve particular societal objectives.

One of the major obstacles in African democracy, constitutionalism and rule of law has been the use of the military and state security organs and also the use of state resources in suffocating democracy, rule of law and constitutionalism. There is no state that can maintain its power and continue over a very long time through the use of force alone. It is therefore recommended that Uganda and other African states must learn to take ordinary citizens along so that the citizens feel that the state is lawfully established with them giving consent, and the rules at least partly serving their interests. This gives legitimacy to the state and legitimacy might rest on different grounds e.g., through a democratic election or through tradition where a state can claim legitimacy through custom but with the consent of the people.

Democracy as a system, may have been with us for so many years, but as a universal value, it is still a new concept and therefore still developing. Depending on one's view, democratic institutions can be seen as enabling or constraining participation. It is therefore recommended that future studies to be conducted will have to investigate further whether it is indeed possible to have a uniform form democratic system in every country in the world.

Conclusion

It was hypothesised that constitutionalism has to be given a wider understanding in accordance with the dynamics of the society, the interpretation should not among others be sought to only look at a government with a constitution or a government established according to the constitution, but a government acting in accordance with the constitution is more important in all aspects, but also not forgetting acting in the interest of the people. Given the findings of this study, the hypothesis has been proven to be correct.

We know that democracy as a system of government has been on the retreat in many countries in the world mainly because of the weaknesses pointed out in this paper. Since democracy is a shifting value, the implication as new politics emerges is that Uganda and other African nations have to find their own conception of politics that can guarantee success and development. the current form of constitutional democracy has in a way hampered Uganda's and Africa's development because the system has so far failed to work well in the African context. In order to deal with the existential threat faced by Uganda and other African nations, it is imperative to identify a system that will work best for Uganda and Africa at large. Democracy should not perceived as 'the only system' that works and therefore enforced as a universal value.

It can be correctly argued that in a way democracy has contributed to the retardation of Uganda and Africa's development because of implementational problems. Democracy as we know it today, is not perfect and has many flaws for example of addressing the majority while at the same time ignoring minority needs. On this basis, it well documented that democracy hasn't successfully worked well everywhere. The only plausible conclusion that can be reached is that democracy and the rule of law are both relative terms and that there are many threads of constitutional democracies rather than a single one that can be referred to as universal value.

As already referenced above, David Bentham is of the opinion that for power to be legitimate, it should not only be based on the three Weberian principles of traditional, legal rational and charismatic authority, but 'it must conform to established rules. Where such established rules are flouted, then it is perceived as a negative implication. The constitution maybe available as a written document, but if it is not [properly performing its functions, it tends to be useless in terms of not being functional. At the beginning of this paper, it was assumed that some constitutional amendments in Uganda are mostly hinged on political power consolidation, political party superiority, and giving the president ultimate power and authority whilst in office. Based on the findings of this study, the assumption is found to be true and consistent as in the case of Uganda and other fragile constitutional democracies.

I am therefore more inclined on the side of Realists' argument that a mere document like a 'constitution' on its own, does not necessarily result into a democracy. The prevalence of a written document is not condition enough to satisfy that a majoritarian democracy is a constitutional state, and neither can the existence of democratic structures a guarantee of the rule of law. In addition to constitutionalism and the rule of law, societal values have to be taken into consideration and encouraged. One of such emerging important value is the idea of human rights. Every person is entitled to certain fundamental rights, simply by the fact that s/he is a human being. They are rights because they are things one is legally and morally entitled to as part of one's existence. They are protected by law and societal values and democracy and participation in politics is an extended right and not an inalienable right.

Much as western democracies emphasise political rights, but the right to life, family etc cannot be taken away in a democratic society as we have seen in some examples where some people are denied a right to family life or forced to break up in perceived constitutional democracies/Monarchs e.g. the UK. The upholding and violation of human rights are all relative ideas in the sense that I might be denied political participation in China but could be allowed family life of which I perceive to be of greater value to me as an individual than political participation. Likewise, I maybe allowed political participation but denied family life in the UK, I may feel that my personal rights have been greatly violated in the UK than in China based on what I perceive as of greater value.

Bibliography

AKIBA, Okoni, "Constitutional Government and the Future of Constitutionalism in Africa." In *Constitutionalism and Society in Africa*, by Okoni Akiba, edited by Okoni Akiba, 3 - 22. Ohio University: Ashgate, 2004.

AKIBA, Okoni, "In Search of Constitutional Order." In *Constitutionalism and Society in Africa*, by Okoni Akiba. Ohio University: Ashgate Publishing Ltd., 2004.

ANDOR, C. T., "Bioethics and Challenges to its growth in Africa." *Open Journal of Philosophy* 1, no. 2 (2011): 67 - 75.

AUSTIN, J., *The Province of Jurisprudence determined*. Edited by W.E. Rumble. Cambridge: Cambridge University Press, 1995.

BERTRAM, Christopher, *Rousseau and the social contract*. London: Routledge Philosophy Guidebook., 2003.

BINGHAM, Thomas Rt. Hon. Lord, House of Lords. *Sixth Sir David Williams Lecture: The Rule of Law*. Online, Nov 2006.

BRAND, James T., "Natural Law and Constitutional Democracy." *The American Scholar* (The Phi Beta Kappa Society) 5, no. 1 (Winter 1936): 5 - 13.

BRAZIER, De Smith and Rodney, *Constitutional and Administrative law*. London and New York: Penguin Books, 1977.

BUSINGYE, Emmanuel, *Kasese Killings: Today marks 4 years as families still wail in pain*. Online: Monitor Newspaper, 6 November 2020.

CHEESEMAN, Nick, "Institutions and Democracy in Africa: How the rules of the game shape political developments." *ResearchGate*, February 2018.

CRESSWELL, J. W., *Research Design: Qualitative, quantitative and mixed methods approaches*. 2nd. CA: Sage Publications, 2003.

EKEH, P., "The Impact of Imperialism on constitutional Thought in Africa." In *Constitutionalism in Africa*, by Okoni Akiba, 25 - 41. Ohio University: Ashgate, 2004.

FEHRENBACHER, D. E., *Constitutions and constitutionalism in Slaveholding South*. 1st. ed. University of Georgia Press, 1989.

FELLMAN, D., *Constitutionalism*. Edited by P. Wiener. Vol. 1. New York: Charles Scriber's Sons, 1974.

FINNIS, John, *Natural Law and Natural Rights*. Oxford: Clarendon Press, 1980.

FINNIS, John, *Natural Law and Natural Rights*. Edited by H. L. A. Hart. Oxford University Press, 1980.

FIORAVANTI, M., *Costituzione* (Translated Section). Bologna: II Mulino, 1999.

FOMBAD, C. M., "Limits on the power to amend constitutions: Recent trends in Africa and their potential impact on constitutionalism." *World congress of Constitutional Law*. Anthens: Online, 11 - 15 June 2007.

FOMBAD, C. M., "Some perspectives on durability and change under modern African constitutions." *African Constitutionalism: Present Challenges and Prospects for the Future*. Pretoria: Oxford University Press and New York University School of Law, 2013. 382 - 412.

FOMBAD, C. M., "Challenges to constitutionalism and constitution rights in Africa and enabling role of political parties: Lessons and Perspectives from Southern Africa." *The American Journal of Comparative Law* (Oxford University Press) 55, no. 1 (2007): 1 - 47.

FREE LAW ESSAYS, *The Rule of Law Origin and Concept*. Prod. Free Law Essays. (accessed 23 July 2019) https://www.lawteacher.net/free-law-essays/constitutional-law/the-rule-of-law-discuss.php

HAGUE ROD, Martin Harrop and SHAUN Breslin. *Comparative Government and Politics: An Introduction.* 3rd. edition. London: Macmillan Press Ltd., 1993.

HART, H. L. A., *The Concept of Law.* Oxford: Oxford University Press., 1994.

HAYEK, Friedrick A., "The Origins of the Rule of law." In *The Constitution of Liberty.* University of Chicago Press, 1960.

HEFFERNAN, Richard, "Governing at the centre: the politics of the parliamentary state." In *Politics and Power in the UK,* edited by Richard Heffernan and Grahame Thompson, 5 - 40. Milton Keynes: Edinburgh University Press, 2005.

HOLMES, Stephen, *Passions and Contraint: On the Theory of Liberal democracy.* Chicago: Chicago University Press., 1995.

HOOD, Laura, *Mali: Top 5 implications of the latest palace coup.* online, 2 June 2021.

HUTCHINSON, Allan C., and COLON-RIOS Joel, "Democracy, Constitutionalism and Judicial Review." *A Journal of Social and Political Theory* (Berghahn Books) 58 (June 2011): 43 - 62.

JUBRIL, B. M., *Concept, Theory and Evolution of constitution Concept Constitutionalism and National Question.* Lagos: Centre for Constitutionalism and demilitarization, 2000, p.16.

KABUMBA, Busingye, *Uganda at 50 and the problem of "Sham constitutions".* Monitor Newspaper. Online, 24 September 2012.

KIBET, E. and FOMBAD, C., "Transformative constitutionalism and the adjudication of constitutional rights in Africa." *African Human Rights Law Journal,* 17, Online, available at: https://www.ahrlj.up.ac.za/kibet-e-fombad-c-2017

LAW, David, S. and VERSTEEG, Mila, "Sham Constitutions." *Cal. L. Review,* 2013: 863.

LIJPHART, Arend, *Democracies; patterns of Majoritarian and Consensus Government in Twenty-One countries.* New Haven: Yale University Press, 1984.

LIKOTI, Fako Johnson, *Challenges of Constitutionalism: Focus on Military Interventions in Three Countries in the 1990s*. Department of Politics and Administrative Studies. No date. https://opendocs.ids.ac.uk/opendocs.

LINCOLN, Egon G. Guba & YVONNA S, *Competing Paradigms in Qualitative Research*. https://www.researchgate.net/ 1994.

LOCKE, John, *Two Treaties of Government*, online eBook. London: Whitmore and Fenn, and C. Brown 1821, 1689.

LOCKE, John, *Two Treatises of Government*. Edited by Peter Laslett. Vols. Cambridge texts in the History of Political Thought, ed. Cambridge: Cambridge University Press, 1991.

LOEWENSTEIN, Karl, "Constitutions, Constitutional Law, Marxism, Communism, and Western Society." Edited by Claus D. Kerning. *A Comparative Encyclopedia* (Online) 11, no. 169 (1972): 174.

LOVELAND, Ian, *Constitutional law, Administrative law and Human Rights: A Critical Introduction*. London: Lexis Nexis Butterworths, 2003.

LOVELAND, Ian, *Constitutional law, Administrative law and Human Rights*. Sixth Edition. Oxford: Oxford University Press, 2012.

LULE, Baker Batte, *Mps Zaake, Nambooze: How we were beaten*. The Observer. online, 4 October 2017.

N. K. SAUNDERS, Mark, LEWIS, Philip and THORNHILL, Adrian, *Research Methods for Business Students*. Eighth Edition. London: Pearson, 2009.

MARKWELL, D., *Constitutional Conventions, and Headship of State: Australian Experience*. Queensland: Connor Court Publishing, 2016.

MAZRUI, Ali A., "Constitutional Change and Cultural Engineering: Africa's Search for New Directions." In *Constitutionalism in Africa: Creating Opportunities, facing Challenges*, by J. Oloka-Onyango, 18 - 51. Kampala: Fountain Publishers, 2001.

MOKGORO, J. Y., "Ubuntu and the law in South Africa." *Colloquium*. Potchefstroom: Konrad-Adenauer-Stiftung, 1998.

MORRIS, Chistopher W., *The very idea of Popular Sovereignty: "We the People" considered*. Online, n.d.

MUHUMUZA, *From Fundamental Change to No Change: The NRM and democratization in Uganda*. Available online (1 September 2009) at: http://journals.openedition.org/eastafrica/578.

MURPHY, Walter, *Constitutionalism and Democracy: Transitions in the Contemporary world*. Edited by Douglas Greenburg et al. New York: Oxford University Press, 1993A.

MUTUA, Makau, "Breaking the barriers: Radical Constitutionalism in the New African Century." In *Constitutionalism in Africa: Creating Opportunities, facing Challenges*, by Oloka-Onyango, 308 - 337. Kampala: Fountain Publishers, 2001.

MUTUNGA, Willy, "Constitutions, Law and Civil Society: Discourses on the legitimacy of people's power." In *Constitutionalism in Africa: Creating opportunities, facing challenges*, by J. Oloka-Onyango, 128 - 144. Kampala: Fountain Publishers, 2001.

NABUDERE, D.W. *Ubuntu Philosophy: Memory and Reconciliation*. Online, No Date.

NEWMAN, I. & BENZ, C. R., *Qualitative - quantitative research methodology: Exploring the interactive continuum*. Carbondale: University of Illiois Press, 1998.

NWABUEZE, Ben, *Constitutional Democracy in Africa*. Vol. 2. Ibadan: Spectrum Books Ltd., 2003.

OJAMBO, Fred, *Ugandan President Secures Sixth Term in Disputed Election*. Bloomberg Newspaper. 16 January 2021.

OKORO, C. B., *Self as a Problem in African Philosophy*. Prod. International Philosophical quarterly. Online: University of Nigeria, December 1992.

OLASUNKANMI, Aborisade, "Constitution without constitutionalism: Interrogating the Africa experience." *Arts and Humanities Open Access Journal* (Medcrave) 2, no. 5 (2018): 272 - 276.

OLOKA-ONYANGO, Joe, "An overview of the legal system in Uganda." *Presentation at the China-Africa Legal Forum*. Makere University: ResearchGate, 31 May 2020. 1 - 7.

PAINE, Thomas, *Rights of man, Common Sense, and other political Writings*. Edited by Mark Philip. New York: Oxford University Press, 1998.

RAMOSE, M. B., ROUX, A. P. J., and TSIE, M. S. S., "Introduction to African Philosophy." *Study Guide*. University of South Africa, 2007.

RUKIRABASHAIJA, Kakwenza, *Museveni said: 'The problem of Africa are leaders who overstay in Power'*. Global Politics Africa. Online, September 2020.

SARTORI, Giovanni, "Constitutionalism: A Preliminary Discussion." *Political Science Review 56*, no. 4 (1962): 853.

SEN, Amartya, "Democracy as a Universal Value." *Journal of Democracy 10*, no. 2 (1999): 3 -17.

SKLAR, Richard L., "Democracy in Africa." *African Studies Review 26*, no. 2 & 3 (1983).

SKLAR, Richard L., "On the Study of Constitutional Government in Africa." In *Constitutionalism and Society in Africa*, by Okoni Akiba, 43 - 51. Aldershort: Ashgate Publishing Ltd., 2004.

STEIN, Robert, "Rule of law: What does it mean?" *Minnesota Journal of Int'l Law* (University of Minnesota Law School) 18, no. 2 (2009): 293 - 303.

TASHAKKORI, A. and TEDDIE, C., *Handbook of mixed methods in social and behavioral research*. CA: Sage Publications, 2003.

TUMWINE-MUKUBWA, Grace Patrick, "Ruled from the Grave: Challenging Antiquated Constitutional Doctrines and values in Commonwealth Africa." In *Constitutionalism in Africa: Creating opportunities, facing challenges*, edited by J. Oloka-Onyango, 287 - 307. Kampala: Fountain Publishers, 2001.

UNKNOWN, *BBI Report pdf and summary (Building Bridges Initiative, Kenya)*. Prod. Kenyayote.com. Online, 13 May 2021. Section 6 (1) HRA. n.d. Online.

UNKNOWN, *Constitutional Monarchy*. n.d. (accessed 03 04, 2021) https://en.wikipedia.org/wiki/constitutional_monarchy.

WADE, A. C. and Bradley, *Constitutionalism and Administrative Law*. London and New York: Longman, 1993, p.4.

WALUBIRI, Peter Mukidi, "Liberating African Civil Society: Towards a New Context of Citizen Participation and Progressive Constitutionalism." In *Constitutionalism in Africa: Creating Opportunities, Facing Challenges*, by J. Oloka-Onyango, 83 - 102. Kampala: Fountain Publishers, 2001.

WALUCHOW, W., "Stanford Encyclopedia of philosophy." *Online Encyclopedia*. 2018. (accessed 01 02, 2021), https://plato.stanford.edu/entries/constitutionalism/.

WARBURTON, Nigel, *Arguments for Freedom*. Milton Keynes: The Open University, 2003.

WASAKA, Anthony, *Uganda ranked worst in rule of law, justice*. Daily Monitor Newspaper. Online, 21 April 2021.

WATSON, L., "The Constitution." In *Politics in Australia*, edited by R. Smith, 51 - 64. North Sydney: Allen & Unwin, 1989.

WU, Chaolan, "Has China lifted 100 million people out of poverty? Yes, it has!" *People's Daily Online*. 6 March 2021. (accessed 04 11, 2021) http://en.people.cn/.

INDEX

DOMUNI-PRESS
publishing house of DOMUNI University

« Le livre grandit avec le lecteur »
"The book grows with the reader."

The University

Domuni University was founded in 1999 by French Dominicans. It offers Bachelor, Master and Doctorate degrees by distance learning, as well as "à la carte" (stand-alone) courses and certificates in philosophy, theology, religious sciences, and social sciences (including both state and canonical diplomas). It welcomes several thousand students on its teaching platform, which operates in five languages: French, English, Spanish, Italian, and Arabic. The platform is accompanied by more than three hundred professors and tutors. Anchored in the Order of Preachers, Domuni University benefits from its centuries-old tradition of study and research. Innovative in many ways, Domuni consists of an international network that offers courses to students worldwide.

To find out more about Domuni:

www.domuni.eu

The publishing house

Domuni-Press disseminates research and publishes works in the academic fields of interest of Domuni University: theology, philosophy, spirituality, history, religions, law and social sciences. Domuni-Press is part of a lively research community located at the heart of the Dominican network. Domuni-Press aims to bring readers closer to their texts by making it possible, via the help of today's digital technology, to have immediate access to them, while ensuring a quality paperback edition. Each work is published in both forms. The key word is simplicity. The subjects are approached with a clear editorial line: academic quality, accessible to all, with the aim of spreading the richness of Christian thought. Six collections are available: theology, philosophy, spirituality, Bible, history, law and social sciences. Domuni-Press has its own online bookshop: www.domunipress.fr. Its books are also available on its main distance selling website: Amazon, Fnac.com, and in more than 900 bookshops and sales outlets around the world.

To find out more about the publishing house:

www.domunipress.fr

EXTRACT FROM THE CATALOGUE

Jean-François ARNOUX,
Et le désert refleurira.

Sabine GINALHAC,
Désir d'enfant. L'éclairage inattendu des récits bibliques.

Pierrette FUZAT,
Un nom au bout de la nuit. Le combat de Jacob.

Patrice SABATER,
La terre en Palestine/Israël.

Marie MONNET,
Emmanuel Levinas. La relation à l'autre.

Apollinaire KIVYAMUNDA,
Maurice Zundel, une biographie spirituelle.

Juliette BORDES,
Viens Colombe. Saint Jean de la Croix.

Joseph MARTY,
Christianisme et Cinéma.

Michel VAN AERDE,
Le père retrouvé

Monique-Lise COHEN, Marie-Thérèse DESOUCHE,
Emmanuel Levinas et la pensée de l'infini.

Claire REGGIO,
Le christianisme des premiers siècles.

Ameer JAJE,
Diaconesses. Les femmes dans l'Église syriaque.

Jean-Paul COUJOU (sous la direction de),
L'État et le pouvoir.

Françoise DUBOST,
L'Évangile des animaux.

Markus JOST,
La Bible à l'école d'Ignace de Loyola et de Menno Simons.

Paul TAVARDON, ocso,
Trappistes en terre sainte. Des moines au cœur de la géopolitique. Latroun, 1890-1946 (T.1).

Paul TAVARDON, ocso,
Trappistes en terre sainte. Des moines au cœur de la géopolitique. Latroun, 1946-1991 (T.2).

Marie MONNET (sous la direction de),
La source théologique du droit.

Nilson Léal DE SA,
La vie fraternelle.

Apollinaire KIVYAMUNDA,
Maurice Zundel. La relation à Dieu.

Lara LOYE,
Fraternités.

Bernadette ESCAFFRE,
Vocations. Quand Dieu appelle.

Raphaël HAAS,
Pleine conscience. Bouddhisme et christianisme en dialogue.

Augustin WILIWOLI,
Axel Honneth. Lutter pour la reconnaissance.

Louis FROUART,
Pascal. Cœur, Corps, Esprit.

Emmanuel BOISSIEU,
Platon. Une manière de vivre.

Emmanuel BOISSIEU,
Kant. Une philosophie de la liberté.

Marie MONNET,
Dieu migrant.

Thérèse HEBBELINCK,
L'Église catholique et les juifs (T.1 et T.2).

Béatrice PAPASOGLOU,
Qu'est-ce que l'homme ?

Augustin WILIWOLI SIBILONI op,
Ce que les philosophes disent du vivre-ensemble.

François MENAGER,
Yves Bonnefoy, poète et philosophe.

Nicole AWAIS,
L'art d'enseigner le fait religieux.

Thérèse M. ANDREVON,
Une théologie à la frontière (T.1 et T2).

Michel VAN AERDE,
Venez vous reposer. Antidotes spirituels au burn-out.

Agnès GODEFROY,
Bien vieillir, dans les pas d'Abraham.

Olivier BELLEIL,
Résolution des conflits dans l'Église primitive.

Anton MILH op & Stephan VAN ERP,
Identité et visibilité. Conflits de générations chez les Dominicains.

Denis LABOURE,
Astrologie et religion au Moyen Age.

Jorel FRANÇOIS,
Voltaire, philosophe de la religion.

Augustin WILIWOLI SIBILONI op,
La reconnaissance. Réparer les blessures.

Jean Baptiste ZEKE,
Loi naturelle et post-humanisme.

Emmanuel BOISSIEU,
Paul Ricœur. Un inconditionnel de l'amour.

Ameer JAJE,
Le chiisme. Clés historiques et théologiques.

Jean-René PEGGARY,
L'aube d'une pensée américaine. L'individu chez H. D. Thoreau.

Jean-François ARNOUX,
Comme un feu dévorant. Flammèches d'une lecture incarnée de la Bible.

Olivier BELLEIL,
L'autre dans l'islam coranique.

Sœur Agnès DE LA CROIX,
Miroir juif des évangiles.

Jean-Michel COSSE,
Au centre de l'âme.

Jean-Paul BALDAZZA,
Antoine. Un saint d'Orient et d'Occident.

Ameer JAJE,
Marie dans l'islam.

Olivier PERRU,
Le corps malade.

Jesmond MICALLEF,
Trinitarian Ontology.

Abel TOE,
Pauvreté et développement au Burkina-Faso.

Jude Thaddeus MBI AKEM,
Le développement en Afrique.

Claude LICHTERT,
Lire la Bible ensemble.

Jorel FRANÇOIS,
Voltaire, philosophe contre le fanatisme.

Bruno CALLEBAUT,
Les Évangiles. Leurs origines, leurs exégèses.

Claude LICHTERT,
La parole pour sortir de soi. Dieu et les humains aujourd'hui : parcours biblique.

Heriberto CABRERA REYES,
Effondrement, apocalypse ou renaissance ? Théologie en temps de crise.

Patrick MONJOU,
Comment prêcher à la fin du Moyen Âge ? (T. 1 et T. 2).

Robert PLÉTY,
À la découverte du Rabbi de Nazareth (T. 1).

Robert PLÉTY,
À la rencontre du Rabbi de Nazareth (T. 2).

Jules KATSURANA,
Guide pour la Prévention de la violence sexiste.

Jacques FOURNIER,
La Trinité, mystère d'amour.

Louis D'HÉROUVILLE,
Marie-Madeleine, femme pascale.

Olivier PERRU,
Martin-Stanislas Gillet (1875-1951). La peur de l'effort intellectuel.

Paul-Marcel LEMAIRE,
Vivre l'Évangile.

John Jack LYNCH,
Judith, Sarah and Esther. Jewish heroines.

Paul NYAGA,
Moral Consistency with Lonergan's Thought.

François FAURE,
Emmanuel Mounier : La personne est son engagement (T. 1).

François FAURE,
Emmanuel Mounier : Montrer, sans démontrer (T. 2).

Olivier-Thomas VENARD, Gregory TATUM,
Conversations sur Paul. « Supportez-vous les uns les autres ».

Isaac MUTELO,
Muslim Organisations in South Africa. Political Role Post-1948.

www.ingramcontent.com/pod-product-compliance
Lightning Source LLC
Chambersburg PA
CBHW070845300326
41935CB00039B/1488